100 ACTIVITIES

Based on the
Catechism of the Catholic Church

ELLEN ROSSINI

FOR GRADES 1 TO 8

IGNATIUS PRESS   SAN FRANCISCO

Scripture quotations from the Revised Standard
Version (Catholic Edition)

The Revised Standard Version © 1946, 1952,
and 1957, Catholic Edition © 1965 (NT) and
1966 (OT and Apocrypha) by Division of
Christian Education of the National Council of
the Churches of Christ in the United States of
America

Layout and design by Shoreline Graphics

ISBN 978–0–89870–615–4

Contents

ADVANCED ACTIVITIES

ANSWER KEYS

Introduction

Occasionally in preparing a lesson, a religion teacher needs an extra activity—a short worksheet or a more involved classroom exercise—to convey a message of faith or point of doctrine. At other times, even with good planning, a teacher needs a productive way to engage students for the last 10 or 15 minutes of a class period.

This book was created to help teachers meet these needs. Designed as a supplement for any Catholic catechetical program, it draws its format and content from the *Catechism of the Catholic Church*. The *Catechism* has been affirmed by Pope John Paul II "to be a sure norm for teaching the faith" and an "authentic reference text for teaching catholic doctrine and particularly for preparing local catechisms" (*Fidei Depositum*, 1992).

The classroom activities in this book are numbered 1 through 100 and are arranged into three skill levels: primary (grades 1–3), intermediate (grades 3–5), and advanced (grades 6–8).

Each activity is self-contained and reproducible for classroom use. Few additional materials are required, though student Bibles are often necessary. Most lessons require little advance preparation by the teacher, and most can be completed well within a class period.

Activities for the class as a whole, such as games and discussions, include step-by-step instructions for the teacher. Individual student activities consist of a brief introductory lesson or explanation for the student and an exercise to be completed by the student on his own. The student activities range from simple matchings, fill-in-the-blanks, and multiple-choice questions to more involved Bible research, short answers, and essays. Some exercises may be suitable as tests or review assignments, others as homework or research projects.

The topics of the activities are organized according to the four pillars of the *Catechism*:

> The Profession of Faith
> The Celebration of the Christian Mystery
> Life in Christ
> Christian Prayer

At the top of the page of each activity are the citations of the paragraphs in the *Catechism* (abbreviated CCC) that apply to the lesson. This valuable reference enables teachers to review key doctrinal points as a background for each activity. It is recommended that teachers have easy access to a copy of the *Catechism* and that those teaching older students have an extra copy to make available to the class. Besides being a vital tool for catechetical instruction, the *Catechism* is a beautiful and uplifting summary of our Catholic Faith and is "useful reading for all . . . Christian faithful" (CCC 12).

Naturally, 100 activities are not sufficient to cover the *Catechism* in a comprehensive way. However, this book includes the major points of belief, such as the sacraments and commandments, as well as aspects of the faith that might not be fully addressed in basic catechism texts, such as prayer and Scripture.

It is hoped that these activities will enhance any Catholic religious education program and inspire the faith of students and teachers alike.

E. R.

"I Believe in God the Father . . ."

NAME

Write the names of some things God has created.

1

2

3

4

5

6

Use the letters from the numbered boxes above to finish this sentence.

God is our ☐ ☐ ☐ ☐ ☐ ☐ .
         1   2   3   4   5   6

Our Father

NAME _____

When the Apostles asked Jesus how to pray, the answer He gave them was the prayer we call the "Our Father". By looking at this prayer, we can learn more about the character of the First Person of the Holy Trinity, God the Father. Fill in each blank with the best word from the list below.

| God's | children | Heaven | needs | hears | merciful | good | grace | strength | greater | holy |

By praying this . . .

1. Our Father

2. Who art in Heaven

3. Hallowed be Thy Name

4. Thy Kingdom come

5. Thy will be done on earth as it is in Heaven

6. Give us this day our daily bread

7. And forgive us our trespasses

8. As we forgive those who trespass against us

9. And lead us not into temptation

10. But deliver us from evil

We can know this . . .

1. We are _____ of God.

2. To be with God means to be in _____.

3. God is _____.

4. We want _____ Kingdom of goodness, peace, and joy to spread to all people.

5. God wills only what is _____.

6. God provides for our _____.

7. God is _____.

8. With God's _____, we can and must show love and mercy to others.

9. God gives us free will, but He _____ us when we ask for help to avoid sin, and He gives us _____.

10. God is _____ than the devil.

100 Activities Based on the Catechism of the Catholic Church
© 1996 Ignatius Press

"I Believe in Jesus Christ"

NAME _____

Use the words on the right to complete the sentences.

Jesus is the _____ of God.

He came down from _____.

_____ is Jesus' birthday.

Jesus has a human Mother.

Her name is _____.

God gave Jesus a _____ father.

His name is Joseph.

Jesus came to _____ all people

from their sins.

Jesus came to bring God's _____.

Christmas

foster

love

Heaven

save

Mary

Son

Jesus, Our Savior

NAME

God sent His Son, Jesus, to us on earth so that we could someday come to be with God in Heaven, where we will be happy forever.

The sentences below outline the story of our salvation. Number them in correct **time** order.

☐   Jesus stayed with His disciples for 40 days, then ascended to His Father in Heaven.

☐   God created Adam and Eve in His own image.

☐   Jesus grew up in the town of Nazareth, where He studied, worked, and played; He was loved and cared for by Mary and Joseph, His Mother and foster-father, and He obeyed them.

☐   Jesus was baptized in the Jordan River by His cousin, John the Baptist; for the next three years He healed people, forgave their sins, and taught them about the love of His Father.

☐   Adam and Eve disobeyed God and had to leave the Garden of Eden.

☐   Mary said "Yes", she would become the Mother of Jesus.

☐   God sent many prophets and leaders to prepare the world for His Son.

☐   The Holy Spirit descended upon Jesus' followers on the day of Pentecost, which is known as the birthday of the Church.

☐   Jesus was crucified, died, and was buried; on the third day He rose from the dead.

100 Activities Based on the Catechism of the Catholic Church
© 1996 Ignatius Press

The Name of Jesus

NAME

Use the following number code to complete the sentence beneath it.

A	B	C	D	E	F	G	H	I	J	K	L	M
1	2	3	4	5	6	7	8	9	10	11	12	13

N	O	P	Q	R	S	T	U	V	W	X	Y	Z
14	15	16	17	18	19	20	21	22	23	24	25	26

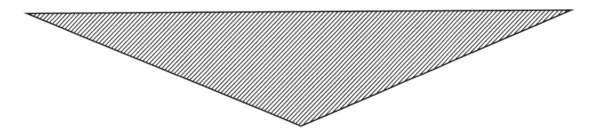

The name "Jesus" in Hebrew means

"— — —   — — — — —".
7 15 4   19 1 22 5 19

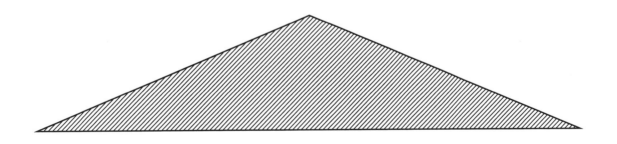

"He Suffered . . . Died, and Was Buried"

Circle these hidden words in the box below.

cross	died	Mary
Jesus	tomb	Good Friday
Pilate	soldiers	buried

```
F   B   X   M   G   L   D   I   S
G   J   C   R   O   S   S   M   L
C   E   M   T   O   M   B   U   F
J   S   A   L   D   I   E   D   A
E   U   R   A   F   R   B   Y   P
S   S   Y   M   R   M   U   L   D
S   O   L   D   I   E   R   S   N
R   T   O   S   D   I   I   D   L
Q   P   I   L   A   T   E   B   U
L   G   Y   S   Y   F   D   X   H
```

PRAY

Jesus, thank You for dying on the Cross to make up for my sins.

Amen.

"On the Third Day He Rose Again"

NAME _____

Listen to your teacher read about Jesus' Resurrection from the
Gospel of Matthew, chapter 28, verses 1 to 10. Then write the
correct word to complete the sentences.

Mary Magdalene and _____ came to the
 (Peter / the other Mary)

tomb. The _____ said Jesus had been raised!
 (guards / angel)

The women were very _____. When they left to tell
 (happy / sad)

the disciples, they met _____. They
 (the angel / Jesus)

_____ His feet.
 (embraced / washed)

The angel and Jesus said the same words to the women. Write
the missing letters in the message.

"D_ n_t be _fr_id."

"I Believe in the Holy Spirit"

NAME

Read the story. Color the pictures.

When we pray, we make the Sign of the ✝. We say, "In the name of the Father, and of the Son, and of the Holy Spirit." Who is the Holy Spirit? We cannot 👁 👁 Him. When Jesus was baptized, the Holy Spirit came down like a 🕊. After Jesus rose from the dead, the Holy Spirit came to Mary and the Apostles as 🔥. The Holy Spirit is with us today in the ⛪. We believe in the Holy Spirit.

Color in the letters.

HOLY SPIRIT

The Holy Spirit

TEACHER-DIRECTED ACTIVITY

Materials: drawing paper, drawing materials.

Directions

Say: Have you ever read a mystery book or seen a detective movie? In such a story a crime occurs, and it is up to police detectives or other investigators to figure out what happened and who was responsible. They didn't witness the event, but through the use of evidence—physical objects, statements from people, etc.—they solve the mystery.

Our Faith teaches us that God is a mystery—the most wonderful mystery we can imagine! We cannot fully understand God. We cannot see Him, but like a detective we believe in God because of the "evidence" He leaves. God the Father is evident in the world, in everything He created. God the Son became evident in the person of Jesus Christ, true God and true man.

What about the Third Person of the Trinity, the Holy Spirit? What "clues" does He leave?

Write the following on the board and discuss one at a time.

> We find the Holy Spirit in:
>
> the Scriptures,
>
> the teaching of the Church through the popes and bishops,
>
> the Mass,
>
> prayer,
>
> the priesthood and other gifted service to the Church,
>
> missionaries who bring the good news of Jesus to all the world,
>
> and in the saints.

Pass out drawing materials, and ask students to draw an example of one of these. Post the drawings in the classroom.

Your Baptism

When you were baptized, you received God's life of grace. You joined the family of God. Circle the things that were part of your Baptism celebration. Color the pictures.

The Sacrament of Baptism

NAME _____

Circle the correct answer.

Baptism takes away sin.
Yes   No

A person can be baptized only once.
Yes   No

Only babies are baptized.
Yes   No

Baptism gives us the Holy Spirit.
Yes   No

The Mass

NAME

Help Father get ready for Mass. Circle the things he will need.
Cross out the things he will not need.

Things We See at Mass

NAME

Match the words with the pictures of things we see at Mass.

Notice them the next time you go to Mass.

ALTAR

TABERNACLE

CANDLE

CHALICE

HOST

LECTIONARY

Preparing to Receive Holy Communion

NAME _____

Choose the correct word or words to complete the sentences.

Before we receive Holy Communion, we must be free from all serious sins;

another name for a serious sin is _____ sin. We can receive God's
                                    mortal / venial

forgiveness for serious sins through the Sacrament of _____.
                                                    Confirmation / Reconciliation

Also before we receive Communion, the Church asks that we fast for at least

_____. To "fast" means that we go without _____
one hour / one night   sweets / food

out of reverence for the Body of our Lord, which we are about to receive. The

Church encourages her people to receive _____ each
                                          Communion / Reconciliation

time they go to Mass. During the first part of the Mass, called the Liturgy of

the _____, we can listen and pray, so that we will be ready
      Eucharist / Word

to receive Jesus' Body and Blood. We can ask for faith to believe that during

the _____ the bread and wine are really
      Lord's Prayer / Eucharistic Prayer

changed into the Body and Blood of Christ. When it is our turn to receive

Communion, the priest or special minister of the Eucharist says, "The Body

of Christ". We answer, _____ to say, "Yes, I believe
                        "Amen" / "Alleluia"

this is Jesus Himself."

Receiving Holy Communion: A Practice Session

TEACHER-DIRECTED ACTIVITY

Materials: unconsecrated communion hosts (one per student), paten or small bowl.

Purpose: to prepare to receive First Holy Communion.

Note: Make prior arrangements to use the church or a chapel for this practice. If possible, meet first in your regular classroom, then proceed as a class to the church. Adjust these directions to local practice, location of tabernacle, and so forth.

Directions

In the classroom, explain to the students that you will be taking them to the church (or chapel) to "rehearse" their First Communion.

Ask: What does it mean to "rehearse" something? [Practice.]

Is a rehearsal the same as the event itself? Is a dance practice the same as the performance? [No.]

Say: That's right. When a man and woman plan to marry, they hold a rehearsal so they can remember what to do and say at their wedding. They aren't married until the actual wedding, when they say their promises, or vows, to each other.

We're going to do something similar today. It's very easy to receive Communion, but sometimes people get a little nervous or distracted by all the excitement of their First Communion. This practice will help you to remember what to do and say. Even with all the attention and special clothes and flowers and pictures, the only really important thing about your First Communion is Jesus and you—Jesus loving you, and you receiving Him.

Since a practice is not the actual sacrament, we will not be giving you the Body of Christ today. I will pretend to be the priest or special minister of the Eucharist, and what I will give you is an unconsecrated host. Has anyone heard the term "unconsecrated host"? [It is a host that has not been changed into the Body of Jesus by the priest at Mass.]

Yes, it means the little wafer of bread that looks like bread, smells like bread, tastes like bread, and really is bread, only bread. When you receive Jesus in the Eucharist, the Host looks like bread, smells like bread, and tastes like bread, but isn't bread at all any more—the wafer has been changed into the Body and Blood, Soul and Divinity of our Lord! Our minds cannot understand it, but our minds believe it.

So, I will say the words, "The Body of Christ" (even though we know this time it isn't), and you will answer, "Amen". You will hold your hands out like a beggar, your right hand cupping your left. I will place the unconsecrated host in your left hand. While facing the altar, you will pick it up with your right hand, put it in your mouth, and eat it. [*Demonstrate this as you speak.*] You will then fold your hands and walk slowly to your pew (or seat), kneel, and say a silent prayer.

Note: If local practice calls for receiving Communion on the tongue, instruct students accordingly.

Say: The time of prayer after Communion is a very special time. You and Jesus are as close as you can be! You can talk to Him about anything. You can listen to Him speak to you in your thoughts. You can praise Him for His goodness and love. You can thank Him for being your Friend and your Savior. You can ask Him to help or heal family and friends. You can seek His help in being a better follower of His. I will lead you in a sample prayer today when all of you have come back to your seats.

Remember, when we enter the church today, that, even though Jesus is not the host I'll be giving you, He is present as consecrated Hosts in the tabernacle. So we honor Him by genuflecting toward the tabernacle before we sit down or kneel. How do we genuflect? Can someone demonstrate? [Call on one child.]

That's right, we touch the right knee to the floor. So, go right up to the first pews (rows), genuflect, move all the way down, and be seated silently. Any questions before we go? Let's line up!

Continued

Receiving Holy Communion: A Practice Session

In the church, you might conduct a brief review of the parts of the Mass. Then, proceed through the practice as you explained to the students. After all have received the practice host, have them repeat after you the lines of this prayer:

> Thank You, Jesus,
> for preparing me to receive You for the first time.
> Thank You for my parents,
> my teachers, and the priest(s) of our church.
> I am so happy that I will soon be so close to You.
> You are great and holy.
> I love You.
> Help me as I grow up so I can be more like You.
> Amen.

Proceed back to classroom, all genuflecting as they leave and blessing themselves with holy water as a reminder of Baptism.

Optional Activity

Distribute copies of page 30 (from Activity 22), "My Prayer". Ask the students to compose their own prayer to say after receiving Jesus for the first time. They may write it in class or take it home for homework.

The Ten Commandments

NAME

Learn this song with your teacher to help you remember the Ten Commandments that God gave us.

Use the tune of "Farmer in the Dell".

Have no gods but Me. (*2x*)
This is the First Commandment:
Have no gods but Me.

Don't use God's name in vain. (*2x*)
This is the Second Commandment:
Don't use God's name in vain.

Keep holy the Sabbath day. (*2x*)
This is the Third Commandment:
Keep holy the Sabbath day.

Honor your mom and dad. (*2x*)
This is the Fourth Commandment:
Honor your mom and dad.

You shall not kill. (*2x*)
This is the Fifth Commandment:
You shall not kill.

Do not commit adultery. (*2x*)
This is the Sixth Commandment:
Do not commit adultery.

You shall not steal. (*2x*)
This is the Seventh Commandment:
You shall not steal.

You shall not lie. (*2x*)
This is the Eighth Commandment:
You shall not lie.

Don't covet your neighbor's wife. (*2x*)
This is the Ninth Commandment:
Don't covet your neighbor's wife.

Don't covet your neighbor's goods. (*2x*)
This is the Tenth Commandment:
Don't covet your neighbor's goods.

God gave us laws of love. (*2x*)
They are the Ten Commandments.
God gave us laws of love.

We Follow Jesus

NAME

Jesus always did what God the Father wanted Him to do. If we follow Jesus, we will also please God and be happy. Match an action you can do with the example Jesus set for us in His earthly life. Connect the dots to match the actions.

WHAT WE CAN DO

Put away my toys. •

Visit a relative in the hospital. •

Play with a younger brother or sister. •

Talk to God during the day. •

Put some money in the collection • for the poor.

Invite a friend to Mass. •

Play with someone who seems lonely. •

WHAT JESUS DID

• *Loved children.*

• *Prayed.*

• *Obeyed His mother and foster father.*

• *Gave people food.*

• *Told people about God's love.*

• *Helped the sick.*

• *Loved people whom others did not like.*

100 Activities Based on the Catechism of the Catholic Church
© 1996 Ignatius Press

We Love God

NAME _____

God gave us the Ten Commandments as His laws of love. The first three tell us how to love God. Write the number of the Commandment next to the sentences that tell ways you can follow that Commandment.

1. You shall not have other gods besides Me.

2. You shall not use God's name in vain.

3. Remember to keep God's day holy.

_____ 1. You go to Mass each Sunday and holy day.

_____ 2. You look up to Jesus more than to sports or movie stars.

_____ 3. You use God's name when you pray to Him.

_____ 4. You talk about God, your Heavenly Father, with respect.

_____ 5. You trust God alone to give you what you need.

_____ 6. You spend some time on Sundays looking at the Bible or other religious books.

PRAY

God, my Father, Your Commandments will help me to be happy with You now and in Heaven. Thank You for Your laws of love.

We Love Our Neighbor

NAME

The last seven Commandments tell us how to love our neighbor.
Write the number of the Commandment next to the sentence
that tells one way to follow it.

4. **Honor your father and your mother.**

5. **You shall not kill.**

6. **You shall not commit adultery.**

7. **You shall not steal.**

8. **You shall not lie.**

9. **You shall not covet your neighbor's wife.**

10. **You shall not covet your neighbor's goods.**

_____ 1. You tell your teacher the real reason for being late.

_____ 2. When you are mad at your brother, you "cool off" instead of hitting
him.

_____ 3. You thank God for the good things He gives you.

_____ 4. You obey your parents.

_____ 5. You ask your dad for the quarter on his dresser before you take it.

_____ 6. You treat your body with modesty and respect.

_____ 7. You are happy with your own family.

_____ 8. You do your chores cheerfully.

_____ 9. You avoid untrue talk about others.

100 Activities Based on the Catechism of the Catholic Church
© 1996 Ignatius Press

The Beatitudes

NAME
_____

Along with your teacher, read the Gospel of Matthew, chapter 5, verses 1 to 12, from the Bible. Then match each action or attitude in the Beatitudes with God's promise for each one.

1. ____ the poor in spirit . . .

    a. shall obtain mercy.

2. ____ those who mourn . . .

    b. shall be comforted.

3. ____ the meek . . .

    c. theirs is the Kingdom of Heaven.

4. ____ those who hunger and thirst for righteousness . . .

    d. shall inherit the earth.

5. ____ the merciful . . .

    e. shall be satisfied.

6. ____ the pure in heart . . .

    f. shall see God.

7. ____ the peacemakers . . .

    g. shall be called sons of God.

8. ____ those who are persecuted for righteousness' sake . . .

    h. theirs is the Kingdom of Heaven.

The Way to Pray

NAME _____

Fill in the last word in each pair of lines to write a rhyme about prayer.

Jesus taught us how to _____.
He wants to talk with us each _____.

At meals we thank God for our _____.
He gives us always what is _____.

At Mass we stand and sing His _____.
For He is God, great in all _____.

We pray for ourselves and the needs of _____.
We pray for parents, sisters, _____.

Prayer can be silent or said out _____.
We can pray alone or in a _____.

To the tabernacle we come and _____.
We believe that Jesus' presence is _____.

The "Our Father", "Hail Mary", and "Glory _____"
Are prayers to be memorized by _____.

The angels and saints are praying, _____.
Praying is good for me and _____!

100 Activities Based on the Catechism of the Catholic Church
© 1996 Ignatius Press

My Prayer

TEACHER-DIRECTED ACTIVITY

Note: This activity may accompany "Receiving Holy Communion: A Practice Session" (Activity 15) or be used as a separate activity.

Directions

Say: Saint John Damascene teaches us that "prayer is the raising of one's mind and heart to God." There are five basic forms of prayer.

Write the name of each form of prayer on the board as you say:

> *1. Blessing and adoration*: We "bless" God or call Him "blessed" because of His love and goodness; we adore Him, that is, we give Him heartfelt love and worship because He is our Creator.
>
> *2. Petition*: We ask God for what we need, especially for forgiveness.
>
> *3. Intercession*: We ask God to help others, even our enemies.
>
> *4. Thanksgiving*: We thank God for all His gifts. Even in difficulty, we ask Him for the good He will bring out of it.
>
> *5. Praise*: We give glory to God just because He is God, not for what He does, but for Who He is.
>
> Now let's see if as a class we can write a prayer using each of these forms.

Go down the list and call on students to give examples of each prayer form. Write them on the board. Then erase the prayers.

Pass out copies of page 30 and say:

> It's your turn to write a prayer of your own, using the forms of prayer you have learned. Simply finish the sentences with your own words.

MY PRAYER

Jesus, I love You because _____

_____

Please forgive all of my sins and help me _____

_____

Also, Jesus, please _____

_____

I pray for _____, who needs

_____

I thank You, Jesus, for _____

_____

I praise You for _____

_____

100 Activities Based on the Catechism of the Catholic Church
© 1996 Ignatius Press

Mary, Mother of Christ

NAME

Our Church has given us a beautiful prayer to Jesus' Mother and our Heavenly Mother. It is the "Hail Mary". Pray it as a class.

The first part of the prayer comes from the Bible. Listen to your teacher read the story in the Gospel of Luke, chapter 1, verses 26 to 45. Raise your hand when you hear the words you recognize from the "Hail Mary".

When God asked Mary to be the Mother of Jesus, she agreed. If you want to be like Mary, color in the X shapes in the picture below to reveal the word you should say when God asks something of you.

Introduction to the Bible

TEACHER-DIRECTED ACTIVITY

Materials: Bibles, one per student and teacher.

Purpose: to begin to familiarize students with the Bible, its basic divisions, and the name of the books that comprise it.

Directions

Distribute the Bibles.

Say: Our Catholic Faith comes to us from two sources, the teaching we receive from our bishops and pope now and back through the ages to the original Apostles—what we call the apostolic Tradition—and Sacred Scripture, the Bible. Does anyone know what the word "Bible" means? [*"Book"—from the Greek language*]

Let's spend a few minutes with the Bible, getting to know it a little bit. Just open it up, anywhere, and read silently for a bit. [*Give students about five minutes for this exercise, longer if they remain focused.*]

Okay, let's share a little about what we read. [*Call on several students. Be open to what they may offer, even if they suggest they couldn't understand what they read—many adults feel intimidated by the Bible. Ask students if they saw any names they recognized, stories they had heard, prayers they know. Discuss.*]

The Bible contains stories, poems, songs, and prayers. For example, our most important Christian prayer comes from the Gospel of Matthew in the Bible. Can you tell me what it is? [*The "Our Father"—Mt 6:9–13*]

Also, the first half of the "Hail Mary" comes right out of the Gospel of Luke in the Bible (Lk 1:28, 42). When we go to Mass, we don't usually bring our Bibles with us. Is the Bible part of our Mass? [*Yes, the Liturgy of the Word—the first part of the Mass—includes readings from the Bible. We can follow along in the missalettes, which have the readings printed for each week.*]

Have your Bible marked at the beginning of the New Testament and at the table of contents noting the books in both the Old and New Testaments. Open up your Bible to where the New Testament begins, to demonstrate the two sections.

Say: The Bible is divided into two main sections. Do you know what they are called? [*The Old Testament and the New Testament*] The first section is the Old Testament, and it contains the story of creation, the history of the Israelites, the Psalms of David, and the prophets—the people God called to prepare the world for the coming of Jesus. Look at the first few pages of your Bibles and see if you can tell me how many books there are in the Old Testament. [*46*]

Now, let's race to find the beginning of the New Testament. When you find the listing of books in the New Testament, tell me how many there are. [*27*] The New Testament contains what? [*The Gospels, the letters of Saint Paul, Saint Peter, Saint John, and others.*] It tells the story of Jesus and the first Christians. Okay, close your Bibles for a minute. I am going to name a book, and I want you to turn to the Bible and tell us whether it is in the Old or the New Testament.

Note: You can go down the row, student by student, so everyone has a turn, or let everyone in class look up the books at the same time, and the first one to raise his hand is called on to give the answer. A third option is a relay race (see Activity 25). Choose books at random, or use the following list:

1. First Letter of John (NT)
2. Genesis (OT)
3. First Kings (OT)
4. Gospel of Mark (NT)
5. Isaiah (OT)
6. Revelation (NT)
7. Joel (OT)
8. Second Corinthians (NT)
9. Acts of the Apostles (NT)
10. Ruth (OT)
11. First and Second Chronicles (OT)
12. Jeremiah (OT)
13. Colossians (NT)
14. Jude (NT)
15. Job (OT)
16. Habakkuk (OT)
17. Titus (NT)
18. Song of Solomon (OT)
19. Galatians (NT)
20. Numbers (OT)

Bible Book Relay

TEACHER-DIRECTED ACTIVITY

Materials: Bibles, paper, pencils.

Directions

Transfer the list of Bible Books (book names only) from Activity 24, Introduction to the Bible, onto two separate sheets of paper. Divide the class into two teams. Give the first player on each team a Bible, one of the lists, and a pencil. The players race to be the first to write "O" for Old Testament or "N" for New Testament next to the name of the book. They may use the Table of Contents in their Bibles if needed. After the first player has finished, he passes the Bible, the list, and the pencil to the next player, who takes the second name on the list. The list passes through the team like a baton in a relay race until all of the books have been designated. The first team to finish the list correctly wins.

Find That Verse

TEACHER-DIRECTED ACTIVITY

Materials: Bibles.

Directions

Divide the class into two or more equal teams, giving a Bible to the first player in each. Call out the first citation from the list at the right to the class. The first players race to find it in the Bible, and when they do they raise their hands. The first to raise his hand is called upon to read the citation aloud. If correct, he earns a point for his team. The Bible is then passed to the second players. The game continues in the same fashion until all of the team members have had a turn. The team with the most points is the winner.

1. 1 John 5:3
2. Genesis 1:27
3. 1 Kings 2:11
4. Mark 12:30
5. Isaiah 12:2
6. Revelation 4:8
7. Joel 2:15
8. 2 Corinthians 13:14
9. Acts 12:1
10. Ruth 1:16
11. 1 Chronicles 16:34
12. Jeremiah 51:15
13. Colossians 3:20
14. Jude 2
15. Job 1:1
16. Habakkuk 3:19
17. Titus 2:11
18. Song of Solomon 2:1
19. Galatians 3:27
20. Numbers 15:40

The Word of God

TEACHER-DIRECTED ACTIVITY

Directions

After your students have been introduced to the names of the books in the Bible and its basic divisions (Old and New Testaments), you can reinforce their knowledge and train their memories to recall the names of the 73 books.

One fun way to begin doing this is by adapting a familiar party game. Have the students sit in a circle and choose one to go first. The student will name a book of the Bible, then add "is the Word of God." For example, "Ephesians is the Word of God." The next student will name another book and repeat the first one: "Genesis and Ephesians are the Word of God." The third will say "John, Genesis, and Ephesians are the Word of God", and so the game will continue, the challenge being to remember the name of all the books said before. If a student gets stumped, you can either have them keep going, or start all over with the next student naming just one book.

As an option, you can do one round of just the New Testament and the next round of the Old Testament. You may also wish to have a list of the books for students to refer to if they cannot think of a book to name, or you could keep the list yourself and cue them if needed.

The Various Books of the Bible

TEACHER-DIRECTED ACTIVITY

Materials: Bibles, copies of the student instruction sheets (pages 35–36).

Directions

This activity is intended as an initial exposure to the traditional subdivisions of the Bible. Some catechism texts may present variations of these categories, or they may group the books differently. If this is the case for your texts, you may wish to adapt this activity to avoid confusion for your students. You can eliminate the introduction given on page 35 and use only the Scripture verses (page 36) in this exercise. You can then replace the category names in the right column with the names your students have learned; or you can write the Scriptures on the chalkboard or a separate sheet and have the students write the names of the categories from which the verses come that they have learned.

The Various Books of the Bible

NAME

You have learned that the Bible is divided into two parts, the Old Testament and the New Testament. You probably are aware that the Old Testament contains the Book of Genesis and tells of Moses and David, while the New Testament features the life of Christ and the early Christians. Beyond that may be uncharted territory.

This exercise is intended to offer a basic map to help you begin to make your way through the 73 different but related books of the Bible and to see how they all fit together. Your travels will last well beyond this year—it can be a wonderful lifelong journey—but this should help get you started.

The Old Testament opens with the five books of the Law (Torah in Hebrew), also called the **Pentateuch**, the most sacred writings of the Jewish religion. They include the story of creation and the great flood, the call of Abraham, the life of Moses, the freeing of the Israelites from Egypt, and the giving of the law in the desert.

After that come the **Historical Books**, which continue the story of the Israelites, beginning with the leadership of Joshua, successor to Moses. These books relate the kingship of David, the rebuilding of the Jewish homeland after exile in Babylon, and, finally, the rededication of the Temple. Tucked in with this history are the books of Ruth, Tobit, Judith, and Esther, each separate stories drawn from this historical period.

The **Wisdom Books**, so called because their purpose is to teach, are in the form of Hebrew poetry and concern the problem of suffering, virtuous living, and the value of wisdom. The lyrical style of the Psalms and the Song of Solomon (Song of Songs) place them in this category, although they are not wisdom literature as such. The Psalms are songs of prayer and worship; the Song of Solomon is a parable in the style of a love poem.

Placed at the end of the Old Testament are the **Prophetic Books**, the writings of God's spokesmen, the prophets. They include the major prophets—Isaiah, Jeremiah, Daniel, and Ezekiel—as well as the twelve minor prophets. The prophets were called by God throughout the history of Israel to preach repentance and, ultimately, to prepare the way for Christ.

Perhaps more familiar to you are the 27 books of the New Testament, beginning with the four **Gospels**. Next comes the Acts of the Apostles, which is a **history of the early Church**, followed by the **Letters** written by Saint Paul and other apostles to various Christian individuals and communities.

The Bible closes with an **Apocalyptic Book**, a story that unveils, using rich symbolic language, a prophetic message from God about the ultimate triumph of good over evil.

The Various Books of the Bible

NAME
_____

Look up the Scripture passages listed on the left. Determine which category given on the right that the book of the Bible belongs in, and write the letter in the space given.

1. Revelation 9:1–11 _____

2. Malachi 3:1–5 _____

3. Philippians 1:1–11 _____

4. 1 Samuel 17:41–51 _____

5. Proverbs 4:10–13 _____

6. 1 John 2:1–5 _____

7. Exodus 34:27–35 _____

8. Acts 12:1–11 _____

9. John 2:1–11 _____

10. Ezra 3:1–6 _____

Old Testament

a. The Pentateuch

b. The Historical Books

c. The Wisdom Books

d. The Prophetic Books

New Testament

e. The Gospels

f. The History of the Early Church

g. The Letters

h. The Apocalyptic Book

100 Activities Based on the Catechism of the Catholic Church
© 1996 Ignatius Press

Abbreviations for Books of the Bible

NAME _____

In written English we use many kinds of abbreviations. For example, we write **Mr.** instead of spelling out **Mister**. We have abbreviations for the names of the books of the Bible. See if you can match some of the names with the abbreviations below.

1. ____ 1 Mac

2. ____ Acts

3. ____ 2 Pet

4. ____ Jas

5. ____ Eph

6. ____ 3 Jn

7. ____ Gen

8. ____ Rev

9. ____ Is

10. ____ Mt

11. ____ Song

12. ____ Ps

a. Genesis

b. Psalms

c. Song of Solomon

d. Isaiah

e. 1 Maccabees

f. Matthew

g. Acts of the Apostles

h. Ephesians

i. 2 Peter

j. James

k. 3 John

l. Revelation

The People of the Gospels

TEACHER-DIRECTED ACTIVITY

Materials: index cards prepared with names and Scripture references, tape, Bibles, paper, three token prizes (e.g., rosary, holy card).

Purpose: to deepen students' knowledge of the people who were touched by Christ.

GAME

Directions

Using the list given below, write one name and its Scripture notation on one side of each index card. Do not show the names to the students.

Say: Today we are going to play a game similar to a party game you may have played before. It's similar to "Twenty Questions" also. Please listen carefully to the directions. I am going to tape to each of your backs an index card with the name of a person from the Gospels. This is your secret identity. The object of the game is to be the first one to guess your identity.

Here's how you play: You mingle around the room and find another student to talk to. You may ask him three questions about yourself that can be answered "Yes" or "No". For example, "Am I a man?" "Am I a disciple?" "Does Jesus heal me?" That student can then ask three questions about his identity. (You look at each other's cards, of course, but not your own.) After three questions, you move on to another student and ask three more questions. You continue like this until you correctly guess who you are.

Note: Depending on how well prepared your students are, you may want to give them a few minutes with their Bibles to scan the Gospels and refresh their memories about some of the people.

Say: Here are a few hints: These are real people, not characters from the stories, or parables, Jesus told. Not every person in the Gospels is known by a name. For example, the Samaritan woman at the well, the one to whom Jesus offered living water, is never referred to by her name but, rather, as "the woman at the well". Also, you might be more than one person, for example, the

soldiers who arrested Jesus. Stretch your memories and your imagination! As soon as you've guessed correctly, come up to me—the first three will get a little prize. Save your cards for the next activity.

People to choose from:

1. Elizabeth, mother of John—Luke 1:39–45
2. Mary, Mother of Jesus—Luke 1:26–38
3. Joseph, husband of Mary—Matthew 2:13–15
4. John the Baptist—Mark 1:2–11
5. Three Wise Men—Matthew 2:1–12
6. King Herod—Luke 23:6–12
7. Peter—Luke 5:1–11
8. Andrew—Matthew 4:18–20
9. James—Mark 10:35–45
10. John, the Apostle—John 19:25–27 (*refers to himself as "the disciple whom Jesus loved"*)
11. Thomas—John 20:24–29
12. Judas Iscariot—Matthew 26:14–16, 20–25
13. A leper—Matthew 8:1–4
14. The faithful centurion—Matthew 8:5–13
15. The paralyzed man—Mark 2:1–12
16. Jairus' daughter—Mark 5:21–24, 35–43
17. Simeon—Luke 2:25–32
18. Rich young man—Matthew 19:16–22
19. Boy with a demon—Matthew 17:14–18
20. Children—Matthew 19:13–15
21. Nicodemus—John 3:1–15
22. Blind beggar—Luke 18:35–43
23. Pharisees—Matthew 23:1–12
24. Lazarus—John 11:38–44
25. Mary, Lazarus' sister—Luke 10:38–42
26. Martha, Lazarus' sister—John 11:17–27
27. Zacchaeus—Luke 19:1–10
28. Pontius Pilate—John 18:28–40, 19:1–16
29. Mary Magdalene—John 20:11–18
30. The good thief—Luke 23:39–43
31. The woman who dried the Lord's feet with her hair—Luke 7:36–50

WORKSHEET

Give each student an "identity card", as above, and a copy of the Activity 31 worksheet (page 39). Each student needs also a Bible and pencil or pen.

The People of the Gospels

NAME _____

Your teacher will give you the name of a person mentioned in the Gospels and the notation for the passage in which the person is mentioned. Using a Bible, read the passage.

Put yourself in the place of the person and think about what it was like to have had a personal encounter with Jesus. Use your imagination to "place yourself" in the Gospel passage and think about how Jesus affected you. Then answer the following questions.

1. Who am I?

2. What happened between Jesus and me?

3. What are my feelings about this experience?

4. What will I do now?

Our Forefathers in Faith

NAME _____

"Now faith is the assurance of what is hoped for and the conviction of things not seen." So begins Chapter 11 of the Letter to the Hebrews in the New Testament. The author of the letter goes on to praise several of the Old Testament fathers of faith, who clung fast to the promises of God even though they did not live to see them fulfilled. This litany of faith encourages us to follow the example of the ancient believers and be hopeful in times of trial.

Read the entire chapter in the Bible, then match the name on the left to the description on the right.

____ 1. Abel

____ 2. Enoch

____ 3. Noah

____ 4. Abraham

____ 5. Isaac

____ 6. Jacob

____ 7. Joseph

____ 8. Moses

____ 9. Rahab

a. Housed two spies sent by Joshua, and so was spared at the fall of Jericho

b. A predecessor of Noah, he was taken up to heaven before his death, a sign of his favor with God

c. Called by God to leave his homeland; though childless, he was promised many descendants

d. Son of Abraham, he also heard God's voice and believed in the promise of a great nation

e. A keeper of flocks who gave God his best lamb as an offering

f. Commanded by God to be fertile and multiply; God sent a rainbow as a sign of his covenant with him

g. Given the name "Israel" after his struggle with an angel; he fathered 12 sons and lived to bless his grandsons

h. Escaped from Egypt, then returned to lead God's people toward the promised land

i. Was betrayed by his brothers and left to die, but came to greatness in Egypt.

100 Activities Based on the Catechism of the Catholic Church
© 1996 Ignatius Press

The Apostles' Creed

NAME

The word "creed" comes from the Latin word *credo*, which means "I believe". The Apostles' Creed is a summary, or short version, of the beliefs of Jesus' chosen followers. The Apostles' Creed is most commonly recited at the beginning of the Rosary, and it is a good one to memorize. When we say the Creed and believe the words we say, we draw close to God. Saint Ambrose called the Creed "the treasure of our soul".

Using the clues below each line, fill in the blanks to complete the Apostles' Creed.

(1) I believe in God, the _____ almighty, creator of
(First Person of the Blessed Trinity)

_____ and earth. (2) I believe in Jesus Christ, his only _____,
(our true home)   (male child)

our Lord. (3) He was conceived by the power of the _____ and born
(Third Person of the Trinity)

of the Virgin _____. (4) He suffered under Pontius Pilate, was
(Jesus' Mother)

_____, died and was buried. (5) He descended into hell. (6) On the
(executed on a cross)

_____ day he rose again. (7) He ascended into heaven and is seated at
(between second and fourth)

the _____ hand of the Father. (8) He will come again to judge the living and
(opposite of left)

the _____. (9) I _____ in the Holy Spirit, the holy catholic
(not living)   (put faith in)

_____, the communion of _____, (10) the forgiveness of
(people of God)   (holy people)

_____, the resurrection of the body, and the _____ everlasting.
(moral wrongs)   (opposite of death)

Amen.

The Nicene Creed

NAME

At each Sunday Mass, after the priest gives a homily, we stand together and "profess our faith", that is, recite a summary of the most important beliefs we share as members of the Church. The profession of faith we make is usually the Nicene Creed. This Creed ("creed" comes from the Latin word *credo*, or "I believe") was composed as a result of two great councils of bishops, held in the cities of Nicaea and Constantinople in the fourth century. Think of it: for sixteen centuries Catholics have professed this same summary of our faith!

Read over the Creed. Then answer the questions on the activity sheet.

. . . .

1. We believe in one God,
   the Father, the Almighty,
   maker of heaven and earth,
   of all that is seen and unseen.

2. We believe in one Lord, Jesus Christ,
   the only Son of God,
   eternally begotten of the Father,
   God from God, Light from Light,
   true God from true God,
   begotten, not made, one in Being with
     the Father.
   Through him all things were made.

3. For us men and for our salvation
     he came down from heaven:
   by the power of the Holy Spirit
     he was born of the Virgin Mary,
     and became man.

4. For our sake he was crucified under
     Pontius Pilate;
   he suffered, died, and was buried.

5. On the third day he rose again
     in fulfillment of the Scriptures;
   he ascended into heaven
     and is seated at the right hand
     of the Father.

6. He will come again in glory to judge
     the living and the dead,
   and his kingdom will have no end.

7. We believe in the Holy Spirit, the Lord,
     the giver of life,
   who proceeds from the Father and the
     Son.
   With the Father and the Son he is
     worshiped and glorified.
   He has spoken through the Prophets.

8. We believe in one holy catholic and
     apostolic Church.

9. We acknowledge one baptism for the
     forgiveness of sins.

10. We look for the resurrection of the
      dead,
    and the life of the world to come.
    Amen.

100 Activities Based on the Catechism of the Catholic Church
© 1996 Ignatius Press

The Nicene Creed

NAME _____

Refer to the words of the Nicene Creed to answer the questions. After each question is the section of the Creed where the answer can be found.

1. What personal name do we use when we talk about, or to, the Almighty God, Creator of everything? (1)

   _____

2. The Son of God was not created by God, as Adam was. In a way that is beyond our human understanding, he comes from the Father while always existing with the Father. What two words in the Creed express this mystery? (2)

   _____

3. Why did the Son of God become man? (3)

   _____

   _____

4. What was the name of the Roman ruler who permitted the crucifixion of Jesus Christ? (4)

   _____

5. What three things did Jesus willingly undergo "for our sake"? (4)

   _____

   _____

6. Jesus' coming, his death, and his Resurrection were not an accident, but part of God's eternal plan. What do we call the writings in which this plan of salvation is revealed? (5)

   _____

7. Where is Christ now? (5)

   _____

8. The first time the Son of God came to earth it was in humility; only those with faith recognized him. When he comes a second and final time, all will recognize him, and his authority will be complete. How will he come? (6)

   _____

9. The Holy Spirit comes from the Father and the Son, yet is just as fully God; the Three Persons are One. What sentence in the Creed expresses this equality? (7)

   _____

10. Through whom has the Holy Spirit spoken? (7)

    _____

11. What are the four characteristics, or marks, of Christ's Church? (8)

    _____

    _____

12. What is the primary sacrament for the forgiveness of sins? (9)

    _____

13. The Christian need not fear his own death nor the end of the world as we know it. What two things do we hope for? (10)

    _____

Memorizing the Creeds

TEACHER-DIRECTED ACTIVITY

Materials: copies of either Activity 33 (the Apostles' Creed, page 41) or 34 (the Nicene Creed, page 42).

Purpose: to guide students in memorizing the Creeds.

Directions

Instruct the students to count off, 1 through 10, repeating the number series as needed so that every student has a number. Give the students a minute to read over the entire Creed silently, and then to concentrate on the statement that corresponds to their assigned number. Beginning with the "Number 1" students and ending with "Number 10", have the students stand and recite their statement. For example, the "Number 1s" would stand and say, "I believe in God, the Father almighty, creator of heaven and earth." They may sit or remain standing, and then the "Number 2s" would stand and recite "I believe in Jesus Christ, his only Son, our Lord."

After one round, have the students turn their papers over and give their statement from memory. Once this is done successfully, you may group some of the numbers together. For example, the 1s and 2s would give the first two statements together; the 3s and 4s recite the third and fourth together; and so on. After that, you could divide them into 1 through 5 and 6 through 10. After this, or in another class period, you can have the students say the entire Creed together from memory.

Spontaneous recitations through the year can reinforce this lesson, as can the praying of the Rosary at home and in class on feast days and other occasions.

Distinguishing the Creeds

TEACHER-DIRECTED ACTIVITY

Game

Directions

Divide the class into two teams. Recite aloud from one of the Creeds. The first team to identify correctly the Apostles' or the Nicene Creed earns a point. Keep score until several rounds have been played.

Silent Activity

Directions

Write or type out the statements from the Creeds onto 20 different index cards (10 for each Creed). Shuffle deck. Students sort cards in order in two rows, one for each Creed.

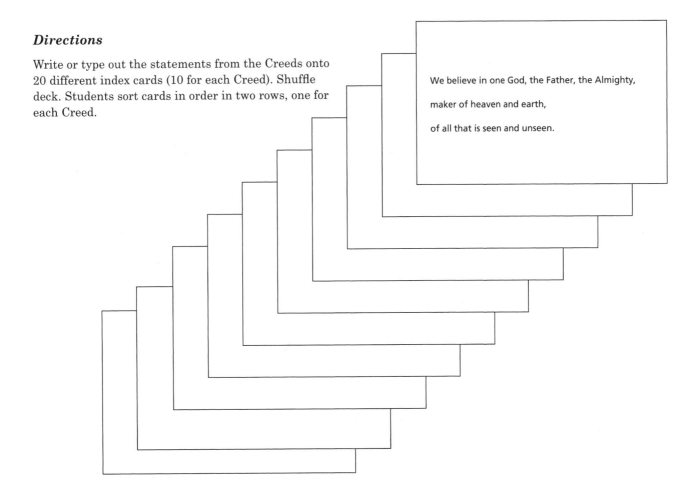

We believe in one God, the Father, the Almighty,

maker of heaven and earth,

of all that is seen and unseen.

The Attributes of God

NAME _____

An "attribute" is a characteristic or trait of a person. Using a dictionary and the Bible, write the definition of each of the attributes of God listed below, and then write the Scripture passage that describes each attribute.

1. **Omnipotent**   _____
   Matthew 19:26   _____

2. **Omniscient**   _____
   Psalm 139:1–2   _____

3. **Sovereign**   _____
   Isaiah 46:9–10   _____

4. **Holy**   _____
   Luke 1:49   _____

5. **Just**   _____
   Isaiah 5:16   _____

6. **Everlasting**   _____
   Exodus 15:18   _____

7. **Wise**   _____
   Proverbs 3:19   _____

8. **Faithful**   _____
   1 John 1:9   _____

9. **Good**   _____
   John 10:11   _____

100 Activities Based on the Catechism of the Catholic Church
© 1996 Ignatius Press

God Is Our Perfect Father

NAME _____

God, our heavenly Father, is perfect: he is all-powerful, all-knowing, and all-good. He made us out of love. One way we can learn about God and his love is through the teaching and example of our human father and mother. Our parents are not perfect, as God is; but they love us, and they try to do what is right.

The sentences below describe the actions of parents. For each sentence, write in an attribute of God the Father that the action can reflect. (An "attribute" is a characteristic or quality of a person or thing.)

**ATTRIBUTES OF
GOD THE FATHER**

**life-giving
just
holy
merciful
kind
wise
generous**

_____ 1. Parents work hard to give their families food, clothing, and shelter.

_____ 2. Parents take special care of their children when they are sick.

_____ 3. Parents give much of their time and attention to their children.

_____ 4. Parents try to do what is right by obeying laws and paying taxes.

_____ 5. Fathers and mothers, joined together with God, bring children into the world.

_____ 6. Parents know and can teach us many things about God and his world.

_____ 7. Parents comfort their children when they are hurt or afraid.

_____ 8. Parents make rules for their children so that they will do what is right.

_____ 9. Parents forgive us when we have done something wrong.

_____ 10. Parents pray and try to follow Jesus' example.

The Story of Creation

NAME _____

Read the first chapter of the Book of Genesis. Then complete the
exercise below by filling in the missing words.

1. The first chapter in Genesis tell us many important truths about God, our Creator.
    From it we learn that God made the world and all living things out of nothing, just
    by willing them to be. "Then God said, 'Let there be light,' and there was light"
    (Gen 1:3). God is omnipotent, or all-_____.

2. We can look at the world around us and see how interesting and beautiful it is.
    Several verses in this chapter tell us that God himself was pleased with what he
    made: "God saw how good it was." A bad musician cannot make good music. A bad
    cook cannot make a good meal. So we can know that, if all creation is good, God, its
    Maker, is all-_____.

3. The chapter we read describes in detail which things God created on each day of the
    week. From this we learn that God did not just throw the world together. He has an
    order, a plan, and design, for his creation. God is omniscient, or all-_____.

4. Genesis reminds us of some very important things about us, too. God did not create
    just one kind of person, but rather, two, which we call _____ and
    _____. Also, God created people to be like himself, not in all ways,
    but in some special ways. We are made in God's _____.

The Days of Creation

NAME

Read the first chapter of the Book of Genesis. Then match the created thing with the creation day by drawing a connecting line or arrow.

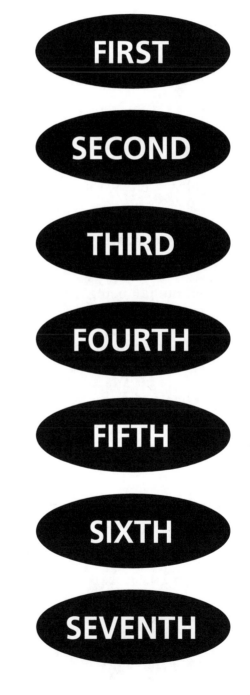

The Angels

NAME

True or False

Circle the correct answer for each statement.

1. Like human beings, angels have bodies.   **True**   **False**

2. Like human souls, angels are immortal.   **True**   **False**

3. The devil is an angel who turned against God.   **True**   **False**

4. Angels watch over us and lead us to God.   **True**   **False**

5. Angels are mentioned all through the Bible.   **True**   **False**

6. When human beings die, they become angels.   **True**   **False**

7. Every person has an angel "assigned" to him.   **True**   **False**

8. Man has a stronger will and greater intellect than the angels.   **True**   **False**

9. Angels are pictured with wings because they are God's messengers.   **True**   **False**

10. Angels do not have free will; they are controlled by God.   **True**   **False**

Name the Angel

NAME _____

1. I am often called "Saint", but I am not a human being; I am an angel. I am even called "archangel", which means I am a leader among the angels. If you see a picture of me, I am usually fighting a dragon; that means that I am in battle against the devil for your sake and for all the Church. My name means "God-like".

   Who am I? _____

2. I have been praying for you and helping you since you were very small. I am mentioned in the Bible, in Matthew 18:10 and in other places. Even before Jesus was born, the Jewish people believed in me and those like me. I am your special friend, and I will help you get to heaven.

   Who am I? _____

3. I have had the privilege of announcing some very important news to some very special people. I appeared to Zechariah to tell him that he would be the father of John, who would become John the Baptist. I told Mary that she had been chosen by God to bear his Son, Jesus. These stories are told in the Gospel of Luke.

   Who am I? _____

The Names of Jesus

NAME _____

Jesus Christ is—first and most important—our Savior, the Son of God, who became man so that he could save us from our sins and return to us the promise of heaven. Yet, in addition to knowing him as our Savior, we sometimes hear and speak of him with other titles and descriptions. Jesus and his followers gave us these other names so that we could more fully understand and think about his love for us.

Fill in the blanks in the sentences below using words from the list at right. Later, you can look for these titles when you are reading the Bible and listen for them in the prayers and readings of the Mass.

| Good |
| Bread |
| Son |
| I Am |
| Adam |
| Light |
| Risen |
| Lord |
| Lamb |
| Man |

1. Jesus always referred to God as "my Father"; therefore, he identifies himself as the _____ of God.

2. Because his obedience made up in a glorious way for the disobedience of the first man, Adam, Jesus is a kind of New _____.

3. During his public ministry, Jesus demonstrated through miracles (healings, calming the storm, raising the dead) that he is the _____, or master, of creation.

4. Jesus died, was buried, and rose from the dead. He is alive today as the _____ One, in whom we hope for our own resurrection.

5. In Holy Communion, Jesus is revealed by faith as the _____ of Life.

6. During the Passover, the Israelite slaves in Egypt killed a young sheep or goat and put its blood on their doorposts so death would "pass over" them. Jesus became the new and perfect _____ of God by shedding his blood and "covering" all believers so they would be spared from the slavery of sin and separation from God.

7. By calling himself the Son of _____, Jesus expressed the truth that he is fully human and came to serve mankind.

8. Jesus Christ "lay down his life for his sheep". He not only guides us and protects our souls from danger, he actually died so we could live. He is the _____ Shepherd.

9. Jesus is truly God, therefore, he can call himself by the name that God revealed to Moses: "Yahweh", or "_____".

10. Before Jesus came, the world was in spiritual darkness because of sin. Jesus is now the _____ of the world.

The Consoler

NAME _____

In the Gospel of John, Jesus tells his followers about the Holy Spirit, who will come to them after Jesus goes to be with his Father. Jesus uses a special name to describe the Holy Spirit. The name means "he who is called to one's side", or "consoler". Discover this special name by filling in the blanks below and placing the boxed letters in order at the bottom of the page.

1. ☐ _ _ _ _ _ _ _ _

2. ☐ _ _ _ _ _ _ _

3. _ _ ☐ _

4. _ _ _ _ _ ☐ _

5. _ _ _ _ ☐ _

6. _ _ ☐ _
   _ _ _ _ _

7. _ _ _ ☐ _

8. _ _ _ _ _ ☐ _ _ _

9. _ _ _ ☐

1. This feast marks the beginning of the Church, when the Holy Spirit came upon the disciples in the form of tongues of fire.

2. Through the power of the Holy Spirit, these chosen followers of Jesus were able to work healing miracles as Jesus did.

3. This faithful daughter of Israel was specially prepared by the Holy Spirit to become the Mother of God.

4. This great father of the faith experienced the power of the Holy Spirit with God's promise that he would be the father of a whole nation, even though he and his wife Sarah were childless.

5. We believe the Holy Spirit, in union with the Father and Son, guides the Catholic _____.

6. This Person of the Blessed Trinity came into your soul at your Baptism.

7. This symbol of the Holy Spirit is used in the Sacrament of Baptism and reminds us of being washed clean.

8. The Holy Spirit inspired the writing of, and continues to speak to us through, the Bible, also known as Sacred _____.

9. This traditional symbol of the Spirit is the form in which he appeared over Jesus after his baptism.

The name Jesus used for the Holy Spirit is _ _ _ _ _ _ _ _ _.

1   2   3   4   5   6   7   8   9

The Fruits of the Holy Spirit

NAME

God pours out his love to us through the Holy Spirit, whom we received at our Baptism. It is through the Holy Spirit that our sins are forgiven and God's life in us can shine, bringing his love to others. Saint Paul wrote about nine ways that God's grace is evident in our lives. We call them the "fruits of the Spirit".

To illustrate how sin can cover up these fruits, the names of the fruits have been disguised in a code. Follow the instructions below to "break through" sin and reveal the fruits of the Spirit for all to see!

The code breaker at right is designed like the key pad of a telephone. As you can see, most of the letters of the alphabet (except Q and Z) correspond to a number on the pad. The number alone won't tell you which letter to use in each group, however. So the code is as follows:

A number alone equals the first letter of a group (2 = A).
A number underlined equals the second letter (2 = B).
A number with a bar through it equals the third letter (2 = C).

Using this code, you find that the fruits of the Spirit are:

Phone Code		
	ABC	DEF
1	2	3
GHI	JKL	MNO
4	5	6
PRS	TUV	WXY
7	8	9
*	0	#

5 6 8 3   _____

5 6 9   _____

7 3 2 2 3   _____

7 2 8 4 3 6 2 3   _____

5 4 6 3 6 3 7 7   _____

4 6 6 3 6 3 7 7   _____

3 2 4 8 4 3 8 5 6 3 7 7   _____

4 3 6 8 5 3 6 3 7 7   _____

7 3 5 3 – 2 6 6 8 7 6 5   _____

The Four Marks of the Church

At each Sunday Mass, when we say the Nicene Creed, we state four things we believe about the Church. We say the Church is one, holy, catholic, and apostolic. We call these the "marks", or characteristics, of the Church. This activity will explore these four characteristics.

For each sentence, write the letter for the "mark" that best fits.

O = One   **H** = Holy   **C** = Catholic   **A** = Apostolic

_____ 1. The source of the Church is God himself, the mysterious unity of Three Persons in one God: Father, Son, and Holy Spirit.

_____ 2. Through the pope, bishops, and priests, the Church continues the mission Jesus gave his chosen followers: "As the Father has sent me, even so I send you."

_____ 3. Catholics all over the world profess the same faith.

_____ 4. The members of the Church, the People of God, are called saints.

_____ 5. Jesus invites all people to become fully his within the Catholic Church.

_____ 6. The Church "canonizes" certain of its members; that is, we recognize as models those Christians who practiced heroic virtue and faithfulness to God and who now dwell with him in heaven.

_____ 7. Where there are divisions among Christians, the Holy Spirit inspires us to pray and work for unity.

_____ 8. The Church is "universal" because she received from Christ all that is needed for salvation.

_____ 9. All members of the Church share in the work of the first Apostles to spread the good news of Christ.

_____ 10. The Church is sanctified by Christ.

_____ 11. Each particular Catholic church, that is, each diocese, is in communion with the Church of Rome.

_____ 12. The Holy Spirit dwells in the Church to ensure the continuous teaching Jesus gave to the Twelve.

The Church Is Apostolic / Names of the Apostles

TEACHER-DIRECTED ACTIVITY

Materials: chalkboard, chalk and eraser, Bibles.

Purpose: to teach the fourth mark, "apostolic"; names of the Apostles with memory aid.

Directions

Say: When we say the Nicene Creed each Sunday, we recite what we call the four "marks", or characteristics, of the Church. Say it with me: "We believe in one holy catholic and apostolic church." The Church is one, it is holy, it is catholic, and it is apostolic. [*Raise one finger for each mark as you say them.*] In this activity, we will focus on the fourth mark: apostolic. What word do you see inside this word "apostolic"? [*Write it out on the board. Listen for or provide the answer, "apostle", and then write it directly underneath.*] What do the apostles have to do with the Church? [*Affirm such answers as: They were chosen by Christ; they started the Church.*] Jesus built the Church beginning with the Twelve Apostles. He asked them to follow him, he taught them about God and his plan to save the world through himself, and after he ascended to the Father he sent them the Holy Spirit so they could carry on his mission. Now that all the Apostles have died and are in heaven, who has taken their place? [*Listen for: priests, the pope, bishops.*] That's right, the bishops, together with the pope and assisted by priests—they are the successors of the Apostles, the ones who come after them to continue their

work. That is why we say the Church is apostolic—it is founded on the Apostles and continues their mission. Every member of the Church shares in the apostolic mission, each in his own way.

Now, who can tell me the names of the Twelve Apostles? Tell me as many as you can think of. [*Write them on board.*] I want to teach you a couple of tricks that may help you remember all twelve. For one, the names of the Apostles are all together in one place in the Gospel of Matthew, Chapter 10, beginning with verse 2. Now, how will you remember that? Well, Matthew is an Apostle, and 10 plus 2 equals 12. Right now, let's look it up in our Bibles.

Now, here is the other trick. [*Write BAPTISM out on board, with space between and below the letters—see chart below.*] If you think of the "I" as "J", then all the names of the Apostles can fit into this word like an acrostic. Let's try it. Which Apostle's name starts with the letter "B"?

As students call out "Bartholomew", write it out underneath the "B". Continue this way until the board looks as shown below.

Give students time to copy this list in their notebooks or on paper. (Prior to that, if time allows, you may erase the Apostles' names, have students close their Bibles, and see how many they can remember on their own.)

B	A	P	T	I	S	M
Bartholomew	Andrew	Peter	Thomas	James	Simon	Matthew
		Philip	Thaddeus	James		
				John		
				Judas		

The Parts of the Mass

TEACHER-DIRECTED ACTIVITIES

Materials: flashcards prepared from page 58, chalk, chalkboard.

Purpose: To increase students' understanding of the various elements in the Eucharistic celebration.

Game I

Directions

To make flash cards, photocopy page 58 onto heavy paper and cut apart. Or cut apart and paste onto index cards.

Make two columns on the chalkboard, labeling one "A" and the other "B". In each column write the following words, but list them in different order in each column:

> Homily
> Gathering
> Intercessions
> Penitential Rite
> Eucharistic Prayer
> Second Reading
> Liturgy of the Eucharist
> Rite of Peace
> Liturgy of the Word
> First Reading
> Offertory
> Preface Acclamation
> Memorial Acclamation
> Profession of Faith

Divide the class into two teams, A and B. Place chalk near each column.

Say: Two students, one from each team, will come up to the board at a time. I will read a clue from one of these cards, and you try to identify which part of the Mass I'm describing. The first one to circle the correct answer wins a point for his team. The team with the most points at the end is the winner. Be sure not to get excited and shout out the answer from your seats, or your team will lose the point. We'll take turns, so that for each clue, two different students will come up to the board.

After the game, tell the students that while the Liturgy has undergone changes over the years, the principal elements and order of the celebration have been the same since the first century! Read to them paragraph 1345 from the *Catechism of the Catholic Church*.

Game II

Follow same directions as in Activity 49 except, instead of using cards, read from a missalette one of the prayers from a part of the Mass and have team members try to identify to which part of the Mass it belongs.

Silent Activity

Shuffle one set of the cards made for Activity 49. Have student sort the cards into proper order.

HOMILY
After the Gospel reading, the priest or deacon gives a teaching about the Scriptures and encouragement to the people to put God's word into practice.

INTERCESSIONS
Just before we prepare for the Eucharist, we pray for the needs of the Church and the world.

EUCHARISTIC PRAYER
The summit, or peak, of the celebration, in which we give thanks to God, we ask his blessing on the gifts of bread and wine, and with the words of consecration Christ becomes sacramentally present under the appearances of bread and wine.

LITURGY OF THE EUCHARIST
This section of the Mass includes the Preparation of the Gifts, the Lord's Prayer, the Breaking of the Bread, and Communion.

LITURGY OF THE WORD
This follows the "Glory to God" prayer and includes readings from the Scriptures.

OFFERTORY
The bread and wine are brought to the altar, and contributions to the church and for the poor are collected from those assembled.

MEMORIAL ACCLAMATION
This prayer, spoken by the people during the Eucharistic Prayer, is a remembrance of Jesus' death, Resurrection, and promise of his return.

GATHERING
Christians come together in one place to worship God and receive Christ in the Eucharist. This time is often celebrated with a song.

PENITENTIAL RITE
Before we listen to the Word of God, we make a prayer to confess our sins and ask the Lord's mercy.

SECOND READING
This is from one of the New Testament Epistles.

RITE OF PEACE
The priest begins this with the words, "Lord Jesus Christ, you said to your apostles: I leave you peace, my peace I give to you."

FIRST READING
This comes from the Old Testament, the Acts of the Apostles, or Revelation.

PREFACE ACCLAMATION
Usually known as the "Holy, Holy, Holy", this prayer of praise and thanksgiving comes at the beginning of the Eucharistic Prayer.

PROFESSION OF FAITH
We say the words of the Nicene Creed, which begins, "We believe in one God."

Eucharist: Summit of Our Life in Christ

NAME

Write the answers to the following questions.

1. In attendance at a Catholic wedding are the bride's Uncle Henry, a practicing Catholic; the groom's co-worker Ed, who attends the Methodist church; and Charlene, a neighbor of the bride's family who has no religious beliefs. Of these three, who may receive Holy Communion at the Mass?

   _____

2. Two "dispositions", or conditions, must be present before a person may receive Holy Communion. They are:

   (a) freedom from _____ and (b) a _____ of one hour.

3. Holy Communion produces many good fruits in those who receive. Name one.

   _____

4. How often must a Catholic receive the Eucharist? _____

5. How often may a Catholic receive the Eucharist? _____

6. Why is the Mass sometimes referred to as "the Lord's Supper"?

   _____

7. What does it mean when we refer to "the Holy Sacrifice" or "sacrifice of the Mass"?

   _____

8. During the Eucharistic Prayer, the priest says the words of Jesus that change the bread and wine into his Body and Blood. What are these words called?

   _____

9. The word "Eucharist" means "thanksgiving". For what do we give thanks when we celebrate the Mass?

   _____

10. Participating in the celebration of the Mass there may be the faithful, the priest, the deacon, the readers, extraordinary ministers of the Eucharist, and a cantor or musicians. Which of these **must** be there for a valid Mass?

    _____

11. Outside of the celebration of the Mass, how else do Catholics recognize the Real Presence of Christ in the Holy Eucharist?

    _____

Liturgical Colors

NAME

Our celebration of the Eucharist incorporates a variety of words, signs, symbols, and actions. One of these symbols is color. Liturgical colors symbolize the character of the different feasts and seasons of the Church year. These colors are used primarily in the priest's sacramental clothing, or vestments, and in the altar linens; they are also used on banners and other non-permanent decorations.

Below are the four colors in common liturgical use today, with their initials. Match the initial of the color to the descriptions given in Numbers 1 to 4. With that as a guide, match the initials with the feasts and seasons in which they are used, given in Numbers 5 to 13.

W = White   R = Red   P = Purple   G = Green

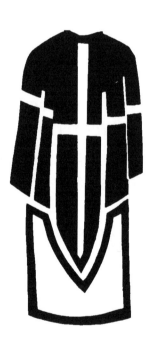

1. Sorrow for sin, repentance, preparation .... _____

2. Hope, growth, life .... _____

3. Joy, innocence, purity, virginity, victory .... _____

4. Sacrifice, blood sacrifice, zeal, Holy Spirit.................... _____

    ⋆ ⋆ ⋆ ⋆ ⋆

5. Advent .... _____

6. Sundays in Ordinary Time .... _____

7. Commemorations of Jesus' Passion .... _____

8. Feasts of Mary .... _____

9. Lent .... _____

10. Masses for martyrs .... _____

11. Christmas .... _____

12. Pentecost .... _____

13. Easter .... _____

100 Activities Based on the Catechism of the Catholic Church
© 1996 Ignatius Press

Vocations: The Sacrament of Holy Orders

NAME

Circle True or False

1. The sign of the Sacrament of Holy Orders is the laying on of hands by the bishop. **True   False**

2. In imitation of Christ and of his Twelve Apostles, who chose men as successors, only men may be ordained. **True   False**

3. When a priest retires from active service, he ceases to be a priest. **True   False**

4. Deacons are allowed to assist the priest and bishop by blessing marriages. **True   False**

5. The three degrees of ordination are episcopate (bishop), presbyterate (priest), and diaconate (deacon). **True   False**

6. Christ is present to the Church in the service of a priest, even if the priest commits a serious sin. **True   False**

7. The bishop is the pastor of a particular church, which may include several parishes. **True   False**

8. Priests exercise their ministry separately from the bishop in their own churches. **True   False**

9. Women may one day be priests. **True   False**

10. The work of a priest is to serve the faithful by teaching, offering the sacrifice of the Mass, and leading souls to heaven. **True   False**

11. A religious brother is like a nun, except he is ordained. **True   False**

12. Recipients of the Sacrament of Holy Orders receive a special grace of the Holy Spirit, so they can act as a representative of Christ. **True   False**

Write an Essay

Imagine that a friend of yours who is not a Catholic asks you about our priests. Why do Catholics have priests? What are their responsibilities? Why would someone want to be one? How does someone know if God wants him in the priesthood? Write an essay to answer his questions.

Intermediate • The Celebration of the Christian Mystery — CCC 897–933, 1593, 1597, 1660.

55

Vocations: Following Christ's Call

NAME

Choose the best answer: write its letter (a, b, c) in the blanks.

1. Jesus Christ calls ____ to follow him.
   (a) Catholics
   (b) everyone
   (c) the baptized

2. The first people to be called by God were ____.
   (a) Peter and Andrew
   (b) Abraham and Sarah
   (c) Adam and Eve

3. The Lord is calling us to be _____.
   (a) holy
   (b) friendly
   (c) rich

4. Because the Church is ____, all people are invited to belong.
   (a) holy
   (b) apostolic
   (c) catholic

5. Every person can pray and listen for God's invitation to ____.
   (a) Holy Orders
   (b) the priesthood
   (c) a vocation

6. The main choices for an individual's vocation are to be ____.
   (a) priest or prophet
   (b) priest, religious, or married
   (c) holy or ordinary

7. Those who choose the "consecrated life" of a religious brother, sister, or priest live by the three "evangelical counsels": ____.
   (a) faith, hope, and love
   (b) peace, humility, and joy
   (c) chastity, poverty, and obedience

8. The vocation of the ____ involves bringing Christ into the world of business, government, education, mass media, and so forth.
   (a) laity
   (b) bishops
   (c) religious

9. The work of a religious brother or sister may include ____.
   (a) being the mayor of a city
   (b) praying, teaching, or caring for the sick
   (c) raising a family

10. The Sacrament of Holy Orders is conferred upon _____.
    (a) bishops, priests, and deacons
    (b) popes, cardinals, and priests
    (c) priests, brothers, and sisters

11. The Sacrament of _____ confers an indelible spiritual character, which means it cannot be repeated and it lasts forever.
    (a) Holy Orders
    (b) Matrimony
    (c) Anointing of the Sick

12. The primary tasks of a married couple are_____.
    (a) making lots of money
    (b) assisting the pastor of the local parish
    (c) mutual love and the procreation and education of children

The Family and Society

NAME _____

God did not place you on the earth by yourself. He gave you a family.

Your own family might be large or it might be small, but whatever its size, your family is important. Families are the foundation for all of human society.

Fill in the blanks to see how your family is a building block of the Church and society.

My parents' names are

_____   _____

My name is

_____

My brothers and sisters are

_____   _____

_____   _____

We live at

_____

in the parish of _____   in the city of _____

in the diocese of _____   in the state of _____

We are members of the _____ Church.

We are citizens of the country of

_____

The Domestic Church

NAME

Each Christian family is an image of God, who is a communion of three Persons: Father, Son, and Holy Spirit. Each Christian family is a "domestic church", or home church—a small community of believers who love and serve Christ by loving and serving one another.

Unscramble these words and phrases to show ways your family can fulfill its calling as a "domestic church".

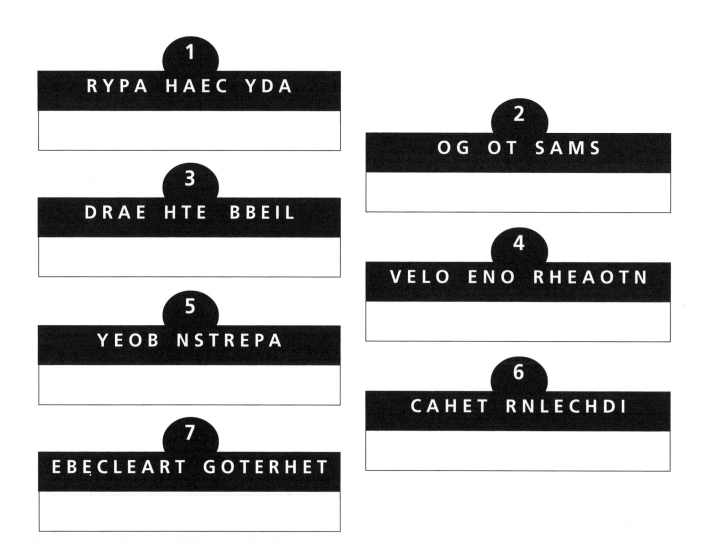

1
RYPA HAEC YDA

2
OG OT SAMS

3
DRAE HTE BBEIL

4
VELO ENO RHEAOTN

5
YEOB NSTREPA

6
CAHET RNLECHDI

7
EBECLEART GOTERHET

100 Activities Based on the Catechism of the Catholic Church
© 1996 Ignatius Press

The Fourth Commandment

NAME

_____

The Fourth Commandment gives us the standard for how we are to treat one another within our family. The Fourth Commandment states:

_____ **your** _____ **and your** _____.

God promised that those who obeyed this commandment would be blessed with a life of peace and well-being. Look up Exodus 20:12 for the exact words of this promise and write them here:

_____

_____

List four ways you can honor your parents:

1. _____

2. _____

3. _____

4. _____

The Ten Commandments: A Scriptural Review

NAME

Printed below is a passage from Scripture that contains the Ten Commandments given to Moses by God on Mount Sinai. This passage is found in the second book of the Bible, the Book of Exodus, chapter 20, verses 2 to 17. Using red and black markers, pencils, or pens, identify each of the Ten Commandments in the Scripture passage in the following ways:

First Commandment:	Circle it.
Second Commandment:	Put a row of dots (. . .) under it.
Third Commandment:	Draw a box ⬜ around it.
Fourth Commandment:	Put an X at beginning and end of it.
Fifth Commandment:	Put a + at beginning and end of it.
Sixth Commandment:	Draw a cloud around it.
Seventh Commandment:	Trace with red marker over its words.
Eighth Commandment:	Enclose it in parentheses ( ).
Ninth Commandment:	Underline it in red.
Tenth Commandment:	Underline it in black.

Hint: The Commandments may be part of a sentence, an entire sentence, or a part of one sentence and all of another. Look hard.

I am the Lord your God, who brought you out of the land of Egypt, out of the house of bondage. You shall have no other gods before me. You shall not make for yourself a graven image, or any likeness of anything that is in heaven above, or that is in the earth beneath, or that is in the water under the earth; you shall not bow down to them or serve them; for I the Lord your God am a jealous God, visiting the iniquity of the fathers upon the children to the third and the fourth generation of those who hate me, but showing steadfast love to thousands of those who love me and keep my commandments. You shall not take the name of the Lord your God in vain; for the Lord will not hold him guiltless who takes his name in vain. Remember the sabbath day, to keep it holy. Six days you shall labor, and do all your work; but the seventh day is a sabbath to the Lord your God; in it you shall not do any work, you, or your son, or your daughter, your manservant, or your maidservant, or your cattle, or the sojourner who is within your gates; for in six days the Lord made heaven and earth, the sea and all that is in them, and rested the seventh day; therefore the Lord blessed the sabbath day and hallowed it. Honor your father and your mother, that your days may be long in the land which the Lord your God gives you. You shall not kill. You shall not commit adultery. You shall not steal. You shall not bear false witness against your neighbor. You shall not covet your neighbor's house; you shall not covet your neighbor's wife, or his manservant, or his maidservant, or his ox, or his ass, or anything that is your neighbor's.

The Ten Commandments

NAME

As you know, the Ten Commandments are in the second book of the Bible, called Exodus. The Ten Commandments are also found in the fifth book of the Bible. The name of this book means "second law", because the book restates and explains the law God gave Moses on Mount Sinai. Both books are part of the Pentateuch, the first five books of the Bible, which hold special significance for the Jews, because they contain all of the laws revealed to them by God.

What is the name of this book? _____

Find the Ten Commandments in Chapter 5, verses 6 to 21, and read them aloud.

Discuss:

1. What did God do for the people of Israel, from whom he demands allegiance and love?

2. What does it mean to take God's name in vain?

3. Why were God's children told to keep holy the sabbath day?

4. What are some ways people might break the Fifth Commandment, without actually taking someone's life?

5. What does it mean to "bear false witness"?

6. God commands us not to "covet" things and people. What does it mean to covet, and what harm can come from it?

The Conscience: God's Voice Within

NAME

The *Catechism of the Catholic Church* defines "conscience" as "a judgment of reason whereby the human person recognizes the moral quality of a concrete act that he is going to perform, is in the process of performing, or has already completed." In other words, each person's conscience operates as an "inner voice" that helps him to know, and choose, right from wrong. Just as our bodies and minds grow, we must also allow our consciences to grow, by nourishing them with the food of prayer, reading of Holy Scripture, and attention to the truths of our Catholic Faith.

Using the following clues, complete the puzzle below.

1. Because God gave us free will, we can freely (??) right or wrong.
2. If we are sure of what our conscience tells us, we must (??) it.
3. Conscience speaks to us as an (??) voice; in order to hear it, we should take time to quiet ourselves in prayer and self-examination.
4. The Holy (??) guides us in the formation of our conscience.
5. Another aid to forming our conscience is the Ten (??).
6. This word means not to know something, to be unaware. This state can cause our conscience to make poor judgments.
7. One rule for choosing rightly is never to do (??), even if good can come of it.
8. (??) is that which offends God; it also offends against a right conscience.
9. The teaching of the (??) can help us form a correct conscience.
10. We need a well-formed conscience in order to (??) God and one another.

1. [C] __ __ __ __ __
2. [O] __ __ __
3. __ [N] __ __ __
4. [S] __ __ __ __ __
5. [C] __ __ __ __ __ __ __ __ __ __ __
6. [I] __ __ __ __ __ __ __ __ __
7. [E] __ __ __
8. __ __ [N]
9. [C] __ __ __ __
10. __ __ __ [E]

100 Activities Based on the Catechism of the Catholic Church
© 1996 Ignatius Press

Growing with the Gifts of the Spirit

NAME _____

At times it seems difficult, if not impossible, to follow Christ and his commandments. We are attracted to his goodness and love, and we want to grow strong in virtue, but we are weak and tempted to sin. How can we do what God asks of us?

Certainly we cannot do it on our own strength, and, fortunately, God does not expect us to. One of the ways he helps us is through what the Church calls the "gifts of the Holy Spirit". The very nature of a gift is that it is free and unearned; so it is with these seven gifts. They came to you at your Baptism and will be strengthened in you when you receive the Sacrament of Confirmation. These gifts help us primarily by preparing our hearts to obey God.

For each gift listed, look up the Scripture reference given. Write the best definition you can find for it in your dictionary. Then, write down a made-up situation that a young person like yourself might face in which the gift could be of help.

1. Wisdom (Job 28:20–28)

Definition _____

_____

Situation _____

_____

2. Understanding (1 Kings 3:4–14)

Definition _____

_____

Situation _____

_____

3. Counsel (Psalm 16:7–11)

Definition _____

_____

Situation _____

_____

4. Fortitude (Psalm 18:2–4, 32–35)

Definition _____

_____

Situation _____

_____

5. Knowledge (Colossians 1:9–13)

Definition _____

_____

Situation _____

_____

6. Piety (1 Timothy 6:11–16)

Definition _____

_____

Situation _____

_____

7. Fear of the Lord (Proverbs 8:13, 9:10, 14:26–27)

Definition _____

_____

Situation _____

_____

Loving Your Brothers and Sisters

NAME

If God has given you brothers or sisters, they are a blessing that is easy to take for granted; or, at times, a blessing you may wish you didn't have! You really do love your siblings; but, because of original sin, they (and you) may not be always easy to live with. By following Christ, you can learn patience with and appreciation for your brothers and sisters. You can be the one to go the extra mile. Then you will be doubly blessed! If you don't have any siblings, you have opportunities to love your cousins, neighbors, and friends. They are blessings, too.

Read each situation below, and imagine yourself as the person involved. How would you respond? What Beatitudes, Commandments, or examples from Christ's life can apply? Write out your answers, then discuss them as a class.

1. Joseph's little sister asks for help with her math problems. Joseph was just getting ready to go outside to play ball. He is afraid that if he doesn't go now, the kids will start the game without him. What would you do if you were Joseph?

   _____

   _____

2. Jack's brother accidentally broke one of his trophies. Jack knows his brother doesn't have the money to replace it. What would you do if you were Jack?

   _____

   _____

3. Twin sisters Tara and Tina tried out for the cheerleading squad. Tara was chosen, but Tina wasn't. One of Tara's shoes has a hole in it, and she asks to borrow Tina's shoes for the first cheerleading practice. What would you do if you were Tina?

   _____

   _____

   _____

4. Michelle is crying in her room because she and her best friend got into an argument. Her sister, Renée, has missed spending time with Michelle, who is always with her friend. What would you say if you were Renée?

   _____

   _____

5. Peter and Theresa want to give their mother a gift for Mother's Day. Peter wants to pool their money and buy her a gift; Theresa wants to make something for her instead. They cannot agree. Choose either Peter or Theresa—what would you do?

   _____

   _____

   _____

The Five Forms of Prayer

NAME _____

All the years that you have been growing up and learning about your faith, your parents, teachers, pastor, and others have encouraged you to pray. You know prayer is a very important part of being a Christian. What exactly does it mean to pray? Is it saying the prayers you have memorized? Is it asking God for help? Is it being attentive at Mass?

Prayer is all of those things, and more.

Imagine your family suffered a big financial loss. You did not have the money to pay your bills or to buy food, and you would have to move out of your house. Suddenly, from out of nowhere, a man started mailing your family all the money you needed for everything and even more. You knew it was real, because you could see the house, the food, the clothes, and the special things you never had before. Naturally, you would want to meet this man. Who was he and why had he done this kindness, you would wonder. You probably would want to say "thank you". You might ask your parents for his phone number, or you might write him a letter.

Suppose, though, that you let some time pass and did not get around to corresponding with the man who helped you. Maybe you hoped your parents would thank him for you. After a while, you stopped thinking about him. You never found out what kind of person he was. You never became his friend.

Without prayer, our faith in God can be like that. We know he is there and deserves our love, yet we neglect to communicate with him. Fortunately for us, God is more than a kind man, and he never stops reaching out to us in friendship. It is never too late to begin to pray.

Holy Scripture and apostolic Tradition have revealed five basic forms of prayer. They are:

Blessing and adoration—returning to God the love we receive from him, and giving him the worship he deserves as our King and Maker.

Petition—asking God for every need, especially for forgiveness and the coming of Christ's Kingdom, but also for every personal need, small or large.

Intercession—praying on behalf of others, even enemies.

Thanksgiving—thanking God for all good things and in every situation.

Praise—giving glory to God not because of what he does, but because of who he is.

On a separate paper, write out the words to the Scripture quotations given below. Identify which prayer form the verse describes or is an example of, and write the **name of the form** next to the verse.

1. Luke 18:13
2. 1 Thessalonians 5:18
3. Psalm 8:1
4. Ephesians 1:3
5. Psalm 9:1
6. 2 Thessalonians 1:11
7. 1 Peter 1:3
8. Revelation 19:1
9. Acts 7:59–60
10. James 1:5

Prayers in the Holy Liturgy

NAME

The Church teaches us that there are **five forms of prayer**: blessing and adoration, petition, intercession, thanksgiving, and praise. We find these forms in the Sacred Scriptures, in our personal communion with God, and in the Mass.

In this exercise, there are three columns. On the left is a phrase from one of the prayers in the Mass. In the center, you are to write the name of the prayer or specific part of the Mass from which the phrase comes. You may refer to a missalette to find the phrases. Then, on the right, identify the **prayer form** of which the given phrase is an example. The first one is done for you.

Phrase	**Prayer / Part**	**Form**
1. Alleluia, alleluia, alleluia.	*Gospel acclamation*	*praise*
2. In your mercy keep us free from sin and protect us from all anxiety . . .		
3. Blessed are you, Lord, God of all creation. Through your goodness we have this bread to offer . . .		
4. We pray to the Lord: Lord, hear our prayer.		
5. May almighty God have mercy on us, forgive us our sins, and bring us to everlasting life.		
6. Father, it is our duty and our salvation, always and everywhere to give you thanks . . .		
7. For you alone are the Holy One, you alone are the Lord, you alone are the Most High, Jesus Christ		
8. Lamb of God, you take away the sins of the world: have mercy on us.		
9. Thanks be to God.		
10. Blessed is he who comes in the name of the Lord.		
11. Through him, with him, in him . . . all glory and honor is yours, almighty Father . . .		
12. Let us give thanks to the Lord, our God. It is right to give him thanks and praise.		

100 Activities Based on the Catechism of the Catholic Church
© 1996 Ignatius Press

Giving Thanks: Counting Your Blessings

NAME

_____

When we think of praying, we often think of asking God for things we want or need. This kind of prayer, called "petition", is only one type of prayer. There are four others: blessing and adoration, intercession, praise, and thanksgiving. This exercise will focus on the prayer of thanksgiving.

At every Mass, we give thanks together: the word "Eucharist" means "thanksgiving". During his ministry on earth, Jesus gave thanks to his Father (Mt 11:25–27), and Saint Paul instructed the early Christians to "give thanks in all circumstances" (1 Thess 5:18).

For what can we give thanks? Everything! We can thank God even for difficulties, knowing that he will bring good out of them. When can we give thanks? Anytime, whether it be after receiving Holy Communion, when we wake up in the morning, or when we go to sleep at night.

God gives us so many good things that sometimes we take them for granted; that is, we expect them and forget to see them as gifts. Making a list of your blessings may help you to see all the good God has done for you. Make a silent prayer as you write:

Thank you, God, for these spiritual gifts (for example, Holy Communion, forgiveness) . . .

_____

_____

_____

_____

_____

Thank you, God, for these special people (for example, parents, parish priest, friends) . . .

_____

_____

_____

_____

_____

Giving Thanks: Counting Your Blessings

NAME _____

Thank you, God, for creating me as you did (that is, with my senses, abilities, gifts) . . .

_____

_____

_____

_____

_____

_____

Thank you, God, for the beautiful world you made (that is, for plants, for pets, for places I have seen or read about) . . .

_____

_____

_____

_____

_____

Thank you, God, for this special prayer you answered . . .

_____

_____

_____

_____

Thank you, God, for bringing good out of this bad situation . . .

_____

_____

_____

_____

This list is for you alone. You may choose to keep it and even add to it.

Praying with the Psalms

NAME

The *Catechism of the Catholic Church* describes the Psalms as "the masterwork of prayer in the Old Testament". Incorporated into the Mass, the Psalms are a part of our communal, or shared, prayer in the Church. The Psalms are also perfectly suited for personal prayer, speaking as they do with genuine human emotion and a simplicity that transcends place and time.

This exercise is intended to help you examine the Psalms in order to increase your appreciation of the Psalm prayers at Mass and in your personal prayers. Read each of the following three passages from the Book of Psalms, and answer the questions.

1. PSALM 23:1–6

a. Where else in the Bible (generally) do we hear God described as a shepherd?

_____

b. If the Lord is my shepherd, what does that make me?

_____

c. Why is that a good description?

_____

_____

d. Describe the mood of this Psalm.

_____

_____

2. PSALM 22:2–22

a. This Psalm opens with a very different mood from that of Psalm 23. Describe it.

_____

_____

_____

Praying with the Psalms

_____

b. Read verses 1 and 17. Of what incident in the Gospels do these remind you? What other verse(s) remind you of this?

_____

_____

c. Many images are used to describe the Psalmist's suffering—bullocks, lions, the sword, and so on. Which image speaks strongly to you, and why?

_____

_____

_____

3. PSALM 96:1–13

a. This Psalm is an example of which form of prayer (blessing and adoration, thanksgiving, petition, intercession, praise)?

_____

b. Was this Psalm likely intended for an assembly or an individual? Why do you think so?

_____

_____

c. This exultation mentions many different attributes of God. Name several of them.

_____   _____

_____   _____

_____   _____

_____   _____

The Rosary

NAME

The Rosary is the most loved of all the special prayers we pray to Mary, the Mother of God and our Mother. The Rosary was revealed to Saint Dominic by Mary herself and was spread as a devotion by Dominican preacher Alan de la Roche in the fifteenth century. Since then, many popes, holy people, and the Blessed Mother have urged Christians to pray the Rosary.

The complete Rosary consists of fifteen decades (a decade is one "Our Father", ten "Hail Marys", and one "Glory Be"). As you pray each decade, you are to think about a "mystery", or special event in the life of Jesus or Mary. The mysteries are grouped into three types: the **Joyful**, the **Sorrowful**, and the **Glorious**.

Below, in the left column, are the names of the fifteen mysteries. The right column contains brief descriptions of each mystery. Write the letter of the description next to the name of the correct mystery.

Joyful Mysteries

____ 1. The Annunciation

____ 2. The Visitation

____ 3. The Nativity

____ 4. The Presentation

____ 5. The Finding in the Temple

Sorrowful Mysteries

____ 6. The Agony in the Garden

____ 7. The Scourging at the Pillar

____ 8. The Crowning with Thorns

____ 9. The Carrying of the Cross

____ 10. The Crucifixion

Glorious Mysteries

____ 11. The Resurrection

____ 12. The Ascension

____ 13. The Descent of the Spirit

____ 14. The Assumption

____ 15. The Coronation

a. After her life on earth is complete, Mary is brought up into heaven by Jesus.

b. Jesus is tied to a pole and beaten with whips.

c. The angel Gabriel appears to tell Mary that she is to be the Mother of God.

d. Jesus crowns Mary as Queen of Heaven and Earth.

e. Jesus prays and suffers the night before he is to die.

f. This event is also known as Pentecost.

g. Jesus rises from the dead.

h. Jesus is born in Bethlehem.

i. Jesus is nailed to a cross and dies.

j. In accordance with Jewish law, Mary presents Jesus in the Temple.

k. Forty days after his death, Jesus goes up into heaven to be with the Father.

l. Jesus is made to carry his cross to Calvary.

m. Mary goes to see her cousin Elizabeth, who is also with child.

n. After Jesus is lost for three days, Mary and Joseph find him in the Temple with the elders.

o. A crown made of thorns is placed on Jesus' head.

The Rosary, Part II

NAME

Connect the letters from Activity 68 **in their final order** to solve the dot-to-dot puzzle.

M •   J •   E •   O •   D •

                                              L •

                                              I •

                              G •   A •

          _____

C •   H •   N •   B •   K •   F •

100 Activities Based on the Catechism of the Catholic Church
© 1996 Ignatius Press

The Hail Mary

NAME _____

Mary is the first Christian and the greatest saint. She was chosen for the most important role given to any created person in history, to be the Mother of Jesus, and she accepted God's will with all of her heart. We believe she is our Mother in Heaven, and, as such, we pray to her, knowing that she loves us, and we pray with her, knowing that she brings our prayers to the heart of Jesus.

One of the Church's favorite ways to pray to Mary is the "Hail Mary". This prayer not only asks for Mary's intercession for us, but also affirms several important truths about Mary and Jesus.

When we pray . . .

1. Hail Mary

2. full of grace

3. the Lord is with thee

4. Blessed art thou among women

5. and blessed is the fruit of thy womb, Jesus

6. Holy Mary

7. Mother of God

8. pray for us sinners now

9. and at the hour of our death

Use these words to complete the sentences

original sin	true man
prayers	Elizabeth
the angel Gabriel	the Cross
conceived	personal sin
our Mother	heaven
the Mother of Jesus	faith
saint	the Holy Spirit

We remember that . . .

1. God sent this joyful greeting through _____ _____ _____, who announced that Mary was chosen to be _____ _____ ___ _____.

2. God prepared Mary for her role by creating her without _____ _____.

3. By God's grace, Mary remained free of _____ _____.

4. Mary's cousin _____ greeted Mary in this way to proclaim Mary's great _____ .

5. By the power of _____ _____ _____, Jesus was _____ inside Mary.

6. Mary is a _____.

7. Jesus is true God and _____ _____.

8. As _____ _____, Mary listens to our prayers and brings them, with her _____, to God.

9. Mary was present with Jesus at _____ _____. She will be with us, too, to lead us to _____.

Sing of Mary

NAME

No woman in history has been more revered or loved than Mary, Mother of Jesus and Mother of the Church. She is the model Christian, having said "Yes" to God through the grace of Christ throughout her life. She is the Queen of All Saints and the patron saint of many countries, including the United States. Truly, as she proclaimed in the Magnificat, "All generations will call me blessed" (Lk 1:48).

The devotion we give to Mary is distinct from the adoration we give God. Though without sin, she remains a created being; God is our Creator and the only One whom we adore. Nevertheless, devotion to the Blessed Mother is not an "add-on" to our faith; rather, it flows naturally from our worship of Christ, her Son and Savior. When we extol Mary, we glorify Christ.

It is no surprise, then, that numerous hymns to and about Mary have been composed and sung over the centuries of Christian worship. They are sung on Marian feast days, other Masses in her honor, and at May crownings. New hymns have been written, and traditional ones remain.

Check the index of your hymnbook(s) for titles that refer to Mary. Examples of some titles you may find are: "Immaculate Mary", "Hail, Holy Queen Enthroned Above", "Sing of Mary", "Song of Mary", "Virgin Full of Grace", "Daily, Daily Sing to Mary", "The Magnificat", "Hail Mary", "She Will Show Us the Promised One", "Mary's Song", "My Soul Magnifies the Lord", "Faithful Love", and "On This Day, O Beautiful Mother".

Read through the lyrics of some of these Marian hymns. You may recognize some favorites, or you may find one you have not heard but whose lyrics you enjoy. Choose one hymn, and, on a separate paper, write a short essay that answers the following questions:

Is the song from, about, or addressed to Mary?

What titles for Mary are used (for example, Queen, Virgin)?

Which attributes of Mary are mentioned (for example, humility, beauty)?

Which attributes of God are mentioned?

Why did you choose this hymn, and what do you like about it?

Note: For this activity, you will need a Catholic hymnal or two and writing materials for a short essay.

My Own Song of Mary

NAME

After reading through some of the Marian hymns (see Activity 71),
write your own song for Mary. (You don't have to write the music, or
sing it!) Think about what titles for Mary you could emphasize, which
aspects of her life you could highlight, or what requests you could
make of her. How can your hymn give glory to God? Remember, a
hymn is essentially a prayer in poem form, with regular stanzas. It may
rhyme, but it does not need to.

Catholic Countdown

NAME _____

Numbers appear throughout the Bible and in our practice of the Catholic Faith. As a brief review of some elements of the faith you have been learning, fill in the blanks of these "countdown" sentences with words given in the list at right. (Not all the words in the list will be used.)

1. Jesus chose **12** men to _____ him and lead the Church as his _____.

2. Only **11** of these men were present at the descent of the Holy Spirit, called _____.

3. God gave Moses **10** _____, which still guide the Church in following Christ.

4. The traditional spiritual practice known as a _____ includes saying certain prayers for **9** days in a row.

5. The **8** _____, taught to us by Jesus, help us to act in ways that will bring us happiness with God now and in Heaven.

6. Jesus instituted **7** _____, through which we receive grace.

7. God _____ the world out of _____ in **6** days.

8. The first **5** books of the Bible, known as the _____, are special to the Jewish people because they contain all of the _____ revealed to them by God.

9. The **4** Gospel writers are: _____, _____, _____, and _____.

10. The **3** Persons of the Blessed Trinity are the _____, the _____, and the _____.

11. All people are _____ of _____ and _____, the **2** people God placed in the Garden of _____.

12. We are made by, and for eternal life with, the **1** _____.

Pentecost
Commandments
Holy Spirit
Matthew
James
descendants
Beatitudes
Eve
Luke
John
novena
rosary
Adam
Father
Pentateuch
Apostles
Mark
pope
follow
True God
created
Eden
saved
Son
laws
sacraments
prayers
nothing

We Believe the Nicene Creed

NAME

The Nicene Creed, recited at every Sunday Mass, summarizes the most important beliefs of the Christian faith. A miniature catechism in itself, some of its components respond directly to certain heresies (denials of essential truths of faith) refuted by the bishops' councils of Nicaea and Constantinople in the fourth century. The Nicene Creed is sufficient to clarify many beliefs that can be contrasted not only with Christian heresy, but non-Christian religions as well.

On the second page of this exercise, match the letter of the doctrinal statement from the Nicene Creed in the left column with the heresy or non-Christian religious belief that it refutes in the right column. Some letters will be used more than once, others not at all.

We Believe the Nicene Creed

NAME

What We Believe

a. We believe in one God,
the Father, the Almighty,

b. maker of heaven and earth,
of all that is seen and unseen.

c. We believe in one Lord, Jesus Christ,
the only Son of God,
eternally begotten of the Father,
God from God, Light from Light,
true God from true God,
begotten, not made, one in Being
with the Father.
Through him all things were made.

d. For us men and for our salvation
he came down from heaven:

e. by the power of the Holy Spirit
he was born of the Virgin Mary,
and became man.

f. For our sake he was crucified
under Pontius Pilate;
he suffered, died, and was buried.

g. On the third day he rose again
in fulfillment of the Scriptures;
he ascended into heaven
and is seated at the right hand of the
Father.
He will come again in glory to judge
the living and the dead,
and his kingdom will have no end.

h. We believe in the Holy Spirit,
the Lord, the giver of life,
who proceeds from the Father and the
Son.
With the Father and the Son
he is worshiped and glorified.
He has spoken through the Prophets.

i. We believe in one holy catholic and
apostolic Church.

j. We acknowledge one baptism for the
forgiveness of sins.

k. We look for the resurrection of the dead,
and the life of the world to come. Amen.

Other Beliefs

___ 1. The Messiah, the one anointed by God
to save us from sin and death, has not
yet come. (Judaism)

___ 2. The world was not created by God but
has always existed as matter.
(Materialism)

___ 3. Jesus is not one with or equal to God
the Father. (Arianism, fourth century;
also Mormonism, Jehovah's
Witnesses)

___ 4. Sins are not forgiven, but are made up
for by our suffering. (Hinduism)

___ 5. Jesus was merely a prophet, as were
Moses, Mohammed, and others.
(Islam)

___ 6. There are many gods. (Shintoism)

___ 7. Christ did not and could not suffer.
(Transcendental Meditation)

___ 8. After death a person is reincarnated,
that is, his soul inhabits another body.
(Hinduism, New Age)

___ 9. Everything is God. (Pantheism, New
Age)

___ 10. Jesus did not have a human nature,
only a divine nature in a human body.
(Gnosticism)

___ 11. Jesus did not rise from the dead. His
disciples merely "kept him alive" by
passing on his teachings. (Some
modern biblical criticism)

___ 12. Salvation from sin results from
seeking an inner peace called
Nirvana. (Buddhism)

100 Activities Based on the Catechism of the Catholic Church
© 1996 Ignatius Press

The Names of God

NAME

What is in a name? According to the *Catechism of the Catholic Church*, a "name expresses a person's essence and identity and the meaning of this person's life". So it is with God's name.

God revealed himself to Moses in the burning bush as "Yhwh", sometimes spelled out "Yahweh". This mysterious name means "I am he who is". Out of reverence, this name is not spoken by the Jewish people, who instead use the name "Adonai"—that is, "Lord", when reading aloud the Scriptures. Through the generations God's people have used other names—many of them linked with "Yahweh"—to highlight different aspects of God's character. In our Christian faith, we can see how these qualities are perfectly reflected in Jesus.

Using your Bibles, match each name for God with the Scriptures where that name can be found.

____ 1. Yahweh Tsidkenu (*The Lord Our Righteousness*)

____ 2. Yahweh Shalom (*The Lord Our Peace*)

____ 3. Yahweh Rapha (*The Lord Heals*)

____ 4. Yahweh Yireh (*The Lord Provides*)

____ 5. Yahweh Shammah (*The Lord Is There*)

____ 6. Yahweh M'Kaddesh (*The Lord Who Sanctifies*)

____ 7. Yahweh Raah (*The Lord Our Shepherd*)

____ 8. Yahweh Sabaoth (*The Lord of Hosts**)

*hosts = an army, or a great multitude

a. Ezekiel 48:35

b. Judges 6:22–24

c. Ezekiel 34:11–16

d. Jeremiah 23:5–6

e. Exodus 15:26

f. Leviticus 20:8

g. Genesis 22:14

h. 1 Samuel 17:40–47

The Names of God Essay

On a separate sheet of paper, write a paragraph explaining which of the above names of God appeals to you most, and why.

Images of the Church

NAME _____

What comes to mind when you hear the words "the Church"? Do you picture the celebration of the Mass? Your local parish and its building, people, or activities? The pope and bishops? The apostles, saints, and martyrs?

The Church is all of these and more. The *Catechism of the Catholic Church* defines the Church as "the People that God gathers in the whole world". This includes the Eucharistic assembly, the local community of believers, and all believers everywhere, on earth and in heaven.

The Church is also a mystery, composed of human and divine, visible and invisible parts. The Scriptures shed light on this mystery by using symbols and images based on everyday human experience to describe the Church. These include a sheepfold, a field prepared for growing, a temple, a bride, and a mother.

At right are given the dominant images of the Church in the New Testament. Look up the Scriptures for each one, and complete the sentence with a quality of the symbol that applies to the Church.

The Body of Christ

Like a body, the Church . . .

1. John 6:55–56 _____

2. 1 Corinthians 12:12 _____

3. 1 Corinthians 12:14 _____

4. 1 Corinthians 12:18 _____

5. 1 Corinthians 12:26 _____

6. Ephesians 4:15 _____

7. Colossians 1:18 _____

The Bride of Christ

Like a bride, the Church . . .

8. Ephesians 5:25 _____

9. Ephesians 5:27 _____

10. Ephesians 5:29 _____

The Temple of the Holy Spirit

Like a temple, the Church . . .

11. 1 Corinthians 3:9 _____

12. 1 Corinthians 3:17 _____

13. 2 Corinthians 6:16 _____

14. Ephesians 2:20 _____

15. 1 Peter 2:6 _____

Images of the Church Essay

Choose one of the images of the Church given above. On a separate paper, write a paragraph examining how the image suitably describes the Church. Develop the analogy; for example, if the Church is like a body, what is its food (Jn 6:55–56)? If it is a bride, who is the bridegroom? If it is a temple, who is the builder? Are there other characteristics in addition to those found in Scripture that also fit both the image and the Church?

The Consecrated Life

NAME

_____

Among the various states in life to which a person may be called by God, the _consecrated life_ offers many opportunities for a person to follow Christ intimately, and thus be a sign of our life in the world to come.

Read each clue, then unscramble the hidden words, which apply to the consecrated life.

1. Consecrated persons make a public profession—that is, a vow—to follow the three

    evangelical counsels, which are: _____, _____, and _____.

Y V R P E T O   T T S A H I Y C   E N E O B I D C E

2. Some consecrated persons live apart from the world in solitude, prayer, and penance. They

    are called _____.

M I S T R E H

3. A consecrated woman who is spiritually betrothed to Christ, and thus becomes a special sign

    of the Church's love for Christ, is called a _____.

I I N G V R

4. Consecrated persons who live together in a common fraternal life under a particular rule, or

    order, are called _____.

U L R I O S G I E

5. To be "consecrated" means to be "_____ _____ for holy use".

E T S   T R A A P

6. Many consecrated persons have been influential in the _____ work of the

S R A S I Y M N I O

    Church, that is, the spreading of the gospel to all the world.

7. Belonging to a secular institute is a way in which Christians can live a consecrated life

    while remaining in _____ _____ and working for its sanctification.

E H T   L W R O D

8. By consecrating himself more closely to God, a person also presents himself to the

    _____ for its good.

R H H C U C

9. Consecrated persons encourage others by their _____. They _____ that

P L X M E A E   E S T I S W N

    our true home is heaven, and the way there is Christ.

A Charade of Saints

TEACHER-DIRECTED ACTIVITY

Materials: index cards, prepared with names from list on page 89; book of saints, such as *Butler's Lives of the Saints* or *The Picture Book of Saints* (Catholic Book Publishing); photocopies of list on page 89, one for each student.

Purpose: to acquaint students with the saints and remind them that these holy ones are alive in Christ and serve him by praying for us. A helpful resource would be a book on the saints, so that some general information can be given during the course of the game.

As the *Catechism* instructs us, the saints in heaven "contemplate God, praise him and constantly care for those whom they have left on earth. . . . We can and should ask them to intercede for us and for the whole world" (2683). Through the years, saints have become known for their special concern and effective prayers for certain persons, countries, or institutions.

Directions

Pass out index cards and lists, one of each per student.

Say: We are going to play a variation on the game Charades. Remember that the object of Charades is to guess what the player is acting out from the player's motions alone; he is not allowed to speak. Sometimes Charades is played with movie titles, books, or songs. Our game is going to be about patron saints.

Have you ever heard the word "patron"? [*It means someone who protects or helps another person; a benefactor.*] What is a saint? [*A holy person declared by the Church to be in heaven because of his exemplary life on earth and the miracles worked through his prayers after his death; also, anyone who has died for the faith.*] So then, what might a patron saint be? [*A holy person in heaven who cares for someone on earth.*]

Over the years, for different reasons, certain saints have come to be known as patron saints for certain people, institutions, or even things. Have you ever heard of praying to Saint Anthony to help you find a lost object? Or perhaps you've learned that Saint Patrick is the patron saint of Ireland, where he was a great missionary during his life. We can at any time ask any of the saints to pray for us, because that is their heavenly "work", to bring our prayers and needs to Christ, with whom they dwell in glory. But it is interesting to learn which saints are believed to have a special love for certain people and circumstances.

You have a list and an index card with names of some saints and those for whom they are patrons. When it is your turn to play, you act out what is on your card, either the saint or the person for whom the saint is a patron. The rest of the class must choose from the list which saint you are charading. For example, Saint Clare is the patroness of television. When Saint Clare consecrated herself to Christ, Saint Francis of Assisi cut off her hair. You could act out someone cutting hair; or you could act out a person watching television or making a TV show. When you've guessed the saint, please raise your hand and wait to be called on, then tell the class the name of the saint and that for which he is a patron— "Saint Clare, the patron saint of television." The first person to make a correct guess is the next player.

Choose a student to begin the game. Proceed as described. After a saint has been identified, you can share some interesting facts with the students such as when and where he lived, what miracles are associated with him, and so forth.

A Charade of Saints

NAME

Albert the Great (*scholar and bishop*) .... scientists
Anastasia (*martyr*) .... weavers
Andrew (*apostle*) .... fishermen
Ann (*mother of Mary*) ....homemakers
Apollonia (*martyr*) ....dentists
Barbara (*martyr*) .... prisoners, architects, and firefighters
Brendan (*missionary*) .... sailors
Catherine of Siena (*advised the pope*) .... nurses
Cecilia (*martyr*) .... musicians
Christopher (*carried the Christ Child*) .... motorists
Clare (*followed Saint Francis, founded Poor Clares*) .... television
Colette (*reformed the Poor Clares*) .... expectant mothers
Dorothy (*martyr*) .... florists and brides
Eligius (*goldsmith*) .... jewelers
Elizabeth of Hungary (*queen*) ....bakers
Frances Xavier Cabrini (*missionary to America*) .... immigrants
Francis de Sales (*bishop*) .... writers
Francis of Assisi (*founded the Order of Friars Minor, also known as
    Franciscans*) .... merchants and animals
Gabriel (*archangel*) .... mail carriers
Gemma (*mystic*) .... pharmacists
Gregory the Great (*pope*) ....singers and teachers
Isidore (*farmer*) .... farmers
Jerome (*Scripture scholar*) .... librarians
Joachim (*father of Mary*) .... fathers
Joan of Arc (*deliverer of France*) .... soldiers and France
Joseph (*foster father of Jesus*) .... carpenters
Joseph of Arimathea (*buried Jesus*) .... funeral directors
Lawrence (*martyr*) .... cooks
Louis of France (*king*) .... barbers
Lucy (*martyr*) .... eye patients
Lydwina (*united her sufferings with those of Christ*) .... skaters
Luke (*physician, Gospel writer*) .... doctors and artists
Matthew (*apostle*) .... accountants and bankers
Michael (*archangel*) .... police officers
Monica (*mother of Saint Augustine*) .... mothers
Sebastian (*soldier*) .... athletes and armies
Teresa of Avila (*reformed the Carmelite Order*) .... headache sufferers
Thérèse of Lisieux (*contemplative*) .... missionaries
Thomas Aquinas (*scholar*) .... students
Thomas More (*lawyer, martyr*) .... lawyers

Which Saint Are You?

TEACHER-DIRECTED ACTIVITY

Materials: index cards and list of saints from Activity 80 ("A Charade of Saints"); three holy cards of saints for prizes.

Directions

Tape an index card on the back of each student without letting the student see the name written on the card.

Say: Today we are going to play a game similar to a party game you may have played before. It's similar to "Twenty Questions" also. Please listen carefully to the directions. I am going to tape on each student's back an index card with the name of a saint. This is your secret identity. The object of the game is to be the first one to guess your identity.

Here's how you play. You mingle around the room and find another student to talk to. He looks at your card, and you look at his. You may ask him three questions about yourself that can be answered "yes" or "no"; for example, "Am I a man?" "Am I a priest?" "Did I found a religious order?" That student then may ask you three questions about his identity. Then you both find someone else to question. You continue in this manner until you can guess who you are. If you need help, I have posted a list of saints on the wall [or bulletin board] to give you some clues. When you have guessed correctly, come to me— the first three will get a little prize.

Patron Saint Biography

Materials: index cards from Activity 80 ("A Charade of Saints"); books about the saints.

Directions

Distribute cards. Explain patron saints (see Activity 80). Ask students to research a saint and write a short biography of his life.

The Resurrection and the Life

NAME

In a group of three or four, take turns looking up these definitions from the *Catechism of the Catholic Church*. Fill in the words being defined.

1. The end of earthly life; the consequence of sin (paragraphs 1007–8).

   _____

2. The reunion of our eternal souls with our transfigured bodies through the power of Christ at the end of time (paragraphs 997, 1001).

   _____

3. The sacrament through which we died and rose with Christ, and henceforth have already entered into his heavenly life (paragraphs 1002–3).

   _____

4. "Each man receives his eternal retribution in his immortal soul at the very moment of his death" (paragraph 1022). This is called the

   _____

5. The "ultimate end and fulfillment of the deepest human longings, the state of supreme, definitive happiness" (paragraph 1024).

   _____

6. "All who die in God's grace and friendship, but still imperfectly purified . . . undergo purification, so as to achieve the holiness necessary to enter the joy of heaven" (paragraphs 1030–31). This state is called

   _____

7. "To die in mortal sin without repenting and accepting God's merciful love means remaining separated from him forever by our own free choice" (paragraph 1033). This is

   _____

8. "In the presence of Christ, who is Truth itself, the truth of each man's relationship with God will be laid bare" (paragraph 1039). This hour is known as the

   _____

9. "Sacred Scripture calls [the] mysterious renewal, which will transform humanity and the world" at the end of time (paragraph 1043) two names:

   _____ and a _____

Articles Used in Worship

NAME _____

The signs and symbols of the Church's celebration of the supreme sacrament, the Sacrament of the Eucharist, include sacred clothing, books, and objects used in worship. Reflecting the long history of the Church, many of these liturgical articles have names with roots in the ancient languages of Latin and Greek.

See how many of the terms on the right you can correctly match with the descriptions on the left.

_____ 1. A square white cloth on which the chalice and paten are placed during Mass.

_____ 2. The priest's outer robe.

_____ 3. Decorative container used to display the Blessed Sacrament for adoration.

_____ 4. Long white tunic worn underneath other priestly vestments.

_____ 5. Person responsible for sacred objects and vestments.

_____ 6. Cloth used to wipe clean the chalice.

_____ 7. Instrument for sprinkling holy water.

_____ 8. Stiff square piece of cloth placed over the chalice during Mass. Also the cloth covering placed over the coffin at funeral Masses.

_____ 9. Strip of cloth worn over priest's shoulders; on a deacon, worn over the left shoulder and crossing to the right side.

_____ 10. Container used to carry Communion to the sick.

_____ 11. Container in which incense is burned.

_____ 12. Readings for the Mass organized by liturgical cycles.

_____ 13. A covered container for consecrated Hosts distributed at Mass or stored in the tabernacle.

_____ 14. Cord used to tie the alb.

_____ 15. Containers for water and wine brought to the altar at the Offertory.

_____ 16. Book used by the priest that contains prayers of the Mass.

_____ 17. Cup that holds the wine that becomes the Precious Blood.

a. alb

b. aspergillem

c. censer

d. chalice

e. chasuble

f. ciborium

g. cincture

h. corporal

i. cruets

j. lectionary

k. monstrance

l. pall

m. purificator

n. pyx

o. sacramentary

p. sacristan

q. stole

100 Activities Based on the Catechism of the Catholic Church
© 1996 Ignatius Press

The Liturgy of the Hours

TEACHER-DIRECTED ACTIVITY

Materials: Liturgy of the Hours prayer books or booklets (one per student or one for every couple of students), available as *Christian Prayer* or *Shorter Christian Prayer*.

Purpose: to introduce students to the "Divine Office", the prayer of the People of God. Praying the Liturgy of the Hours, though commonly associated with priests and religious as befits their calling, is also encouraged for "all the faithful as much as possible . . . either with the priests, or among themselves, or even individually" (*Sacrosanctum concilium*, 1963).

Directions

Invite your pastor to (1) give a guest lecture on the Liturgy of the Hours, to be followed by (2) his leading the students in daytime prayer. A chapel, if available, would be a desirable setting for the prayers; the actual prayer time should take about ten minutes. The priest (or you, with his guidance) will need to prepare materials ahead of time, by marking individual copies of the books so as to lead the students smoothly through the Office.

Questions for the pastor to answer in his lecture might include:

> What is the Liturgy of the Hours?
> Why is it the prayer of the Church?
> Who prays it?
> How is it prayed?
> How often is it prayed, and how long are the prayers?
> How can a layman make use of the prayers—in a family, school, or as an individual?
> What are the major components of the prayer? (Psalms, Our Father, New Testament readings, and so on)
> Is it difficult to learn?
> Why did the Church give us this guide rather than leave it to us to pray spontaneously through the day?

If your parish priest is not available, you could instead invite a deacon, religious brother or sister, or a layman educated and experienced in the use of the Liturgy of the Hours.

Important Days in the Liturgical Year

NAME

The Church calendar marks not the passage of time but various aspects of the Paschal mystery, that is, the mystery of Christ's life, death, and Resurrection. The Church begins a new liturgical year on the First Sunday of Advent. Included on the Church's calendar are solemnities, which celebrate the most significant events, people, and beliefs; feasts, or celebrations of secondary significance; and memorials, which honor martyrs and other saints.

Your teacher will give you a **sample calendar** with some dates circled to mark noteworthy liturgies, including solemnities, feasts, and memorials. For each liturgy named below, write the correct date from among those circled on the sample calendar. (**Note:** Some feasts and solemnities are "movable", that is, their date changes each year. For example, Easter's date is set according to natural cycles of the earth and moon and is adjusted yearly. Likewise, the dates for celebrations that are tied into Easter, such as Ash Wednesday and Ascension Thursday, also change. The date for Easter in this sample calendar is given as April 7.)

For a bonus: Put a star next to the dates of Holy Days of Obligation.

1. Easter   **April 7**   12. Assumption   _____

2. Christmas   _____   13. Saint Patrick's Day   _____

3. Christ the King   _____   14. Holy Family   _____
   (*last Sunday of liturgical year*)

    15. Solemnity of Mary   _____

4. First Sunday of Advent   _____

    16. Annunciation   _____

5. Immaculate Conception   _____

    17. Corpus Christi   _____

6. Pentecost ("*fiftieth day*")   _____
   (*second Sunday after Pentecost*)

7. Ascension Thursday   _____   18. Holy Trinity   _____
   (*Sunday after Pentecost*)

8. Epiphany   _____

    19. Birth of Mary   _____

9. Ash Wednesday   _____

    20. Sacred Heart   _____

10. Good Friday   _____
    (*Friday after Corpus Christi*)

11. All Saints   _____

Important Days in the Liturgical Year

January
S	M	T	W	T	F	S
	①	2	3	4	5	6
⑦	8	9	10	11	12	13
14	15	16	17	18	19	20
21	22	23	24	25	26	27
28	29	30	31			

February
S	M	T	W	T	F	S
				1	2	3
4	5	6	7	8	9	10
11	12	13	14	15	16	17
18	19	20	㉑	22	23	24
25	26	27	28	29		

March
S	M	T	W	T	F	S
					1	2
3	4	5	6	7	8	9
10	11	12	13	14	15	16
⑰	18	19	20	21	22	23
24	㉕	26	27	28	29	30
31						

April
S	M	T	W	T	F	S
	1	2	3	4	⑤	6
⑦	8	9	10	11	12	13
14	15	16	17	18	19	20
21	22	23	24	25	26	27
28	29	30				

May
S	M	T	W	T	F	S
		1	2	3	4	
5	6	7	8	9	10	11
12	13	14	15	⑯	17	18
19	20	21	22	23	24	25
㉖	27	28	29	30	31	

June
S	M	T	W	T	F	S
						1
②	3	4	5	6	7	8
⑨	10	11	12	13	⑭	15
16	17	18	19	20	21	22
23	24	25	26	27	28	29
30						

July
S	M	T	W	T	F	S
	1	2	3	4	5	6
7	8	9	10	11	12	13
14	15	16	17	18	19	20
21	22	23	24	25	26	27
28	29	30	31			

August
S	M	T	W	T	F	S
				1	2	3
4	5	6	7	8	9	10
11	12	13	14	⑮	16	17
18	19	20	21	22	23	24
25	26	27	28	29	30	31

September
S	M	T	W	T	F	S
1	2	3	4	5	6	7
⑧	9	10	11	12	13	14
15	16	17	18	19	20	21
22	23	24	25	26	27	28
29	30					

October
S	M	T	W	T	F	S
		1	2	3	4	5
6	7	8	9	10	11	12
13	14	15	16	17	18	19
20	21	22	23	24	25	26
27	28	29	30	31		

November
S	M	T	W	T	F	S
					①	2
3	4	5	6	7	8	9
10	11	12	13	14	15	16
17	18	19	20	21	22	23
㉔	25	26	27	28	29	30

December
S	M	T	W	T	F	S
①	2	3	4	5	6	7
⑧	9	10	11	12	13	14
15	16	17	18	19	20	21
22	23	24	㉕	26	27	28
㉙	30	31				

Name Days

NAME

In many countries, a child's Name Day is as important a celebration as his birthday. A Name Day is the memorial day of a person's patron saint. If you share a first or middle name with a saint, that saint is your special guardian. Or, if your first or middle name is derived from that of a saint—for example, the names Maggie and Megan come from the name Margaret—that saint is your patron. If you do not know who your patron saint is or do not yet have one, choose a favorite saint to be your patron.

Using Church calendars and books about the saints, find your Name Day and write it here. Then write a paragraph about the life of your patron saint.

_____

_____

_____

_____

_____

_____

_____

_____

_____

_____

_____

_____

_____

_____

_____

100 Activities Based on the Catechism of the Catholic Church
© 1996 Ignatius Press

The Sacrament of Confirmation

NAME

Circle the letter (a, b, c) of the correct answers.

1. Baptism, Eucharist, and Confirmation are united as the
   (a) Sacraments of Preparation
   (b) Sacraments of Initiation
   (c) Sacraments of Unification

2. Confirmation is necessary for a Christian because it
   (a) confers
   (b) replaces
   (c) completes
   the grace given at Baptism.

3. The physical sign of the sacrament is anointing with a perfumed oil consecrated by the bishop. This oil is called:
   (a) balsam
   (b) sanctum
   (c) chrism

4. The bishop consecrates the sacred oil of Confirmation at this liturgy each year:
   (a) Holy Thursday
   (b) Easter Vigil
   (c) Pentecost

5. For the essential rite of the sacrament—that is, the basic and necessary elements of the sacrament—the anointing with oil is accompanied by which other action?
   (a) laying on of the hands
   (b) reception of Holy Eucharist
   (c) sign of peace

6. The essential words spoken by the bishop in the administration of the sacrament are:
   (a) "Go forth and be his witnesses"
   (b) "You are now confirmed"
   (c) "Be sealed with the Gift of the Holy Spirit"

7. The bishop is the ordinary minister of this sacrament primarily because:
   (a) he is a successor to the apostles, who bore witness to Christ
   (b) it is a longstanding traditional practice
   (c) only he is permitted to use the sacred oil

8. Upon receiving the sacrament, the confirmand receives an indelible spiritual mark, the seal of the Holy Spirit, which means:
   (a) he will never commit a mortal sin
   (b) he has received a special power from Christ to be his witness
   (c) his education in the faith is completed

9. Those eligible to receive the sacrament are:
   (a) every baptized person not yet confirmed
   (b) baptized persons who have reached the age of reason
   (c) young adults, whether baptized or not

10. Before receiving Confirmation, one must receive the Sacrament of Penance:
    (a) at least once
    (b) if he has committed a mortal sin
    (c) within one month prior to being confirmed

Anointing with Oil

NAME

As the *Catechism of the Catholic Church* notes in paragraphs 1293 and 1294, the use of oils has a long symbolic tradition, dating to its practical and ritual uses in ancient cultures. The various meanings associated with anointing are integrated into the sacraments of the Church, four in particular: Baptism, Confirmation, Holy Orders, and Anointing of the Sick.

In this activity, you are given some of the physical and symbolic qualities of oil and anointing. For each one, look up and copy the Scripture verse or verses given, then write the name of the sacraments for which the meaning is applicable.

1. **Sign of abundance and joy**

   Psalm 23:5 _____

   _____

   Sacrament(s) _____

   _____

2. **Sign of cleansing**

   Judith 10:1–3 _____

   _____

   Sacrament(s) _____

   _____

3. **Sign of healing**

   Luke 10:34 _____

   _____

   Sacrament(s) _____

   _____

4. **Sign of strength**

   1 Samuel 10:1 _____

   _____

   Sacrament(s) _____

   _____

5. **Sign of beauty (perfumed oil)**

   2 Corinthians 2:15 _____

   _____

   Sacrament(s) _____

   _____

6. **Sign of consecration**

   Exodus 30:30 _____

   _____

   Sacrament(s) _____

   _____

100 Activities Based on the Catechism of the Catholic Church
© 1996 Ignatius Press

A Scriptural Examination of Conscience

Before you receive the Sacrament of Penance, or Reconciliation, you think about your sins. How have your choices—your thoughts and actions—lived up to your call from Christ? How have you kept God's commandments? How have you loved God and neighbor?

We call this process an "examination of conscience". It helps us to identify sins and sinful habits that we can confess to the priest in order to receive penance and forgiveness. We can even do a brief examination daily, so we can be aware of our weaknesses and turn to God for grace and pardon.

Many guides and questionnaires have been written to help us in this examination. Some are based on the Ten Commandments, others on Jesus' two great commandments or the Beatitudes. The rite of the sacrament indicates that whatever form it takes, our examination of conscience should be made "in the light of the Word of God".

In this exercise, you will make your own guide for an examination of conscience based on some key Scriptures. Read each verse, and think about how it applies to someone your age. Then write one or more questions based on the passage to help someone like yourself make a good examination. An example is given below.

(Hint: Some sins are things we do that we should not do; others are things we do not do that we should.)

Matthew 5:22 (on anger)
> *Have I gotten angry with my parents, my brothers or sisters, or friends? Have I used harsh language or profanity? Have I said or done anything hurtful out of anger?*

Matthew 5:28 (on lust)

_____

_____

Matthew 5:43–48 (on love of enemies)

_____

Matthew 6:6 (on prayer)

_____

Matthew 6:14–15 (on forgiveness)

_____

Matthew 6:24 and 2 Timothy 6:9 (on money)

_____

Matthew 7:1–5 (on judging)

_____

Romans 12:16 (on pride)

_____

Romans 13:1–7 (on obedience to authority)

_____

1 Corinthians 13:4–6 (on love)

_____

Ephesians 4:25 (on truth)

_____

Ephesians 4:28 (on stealing)

_____

Ephesians 5:3–4 (on right speech)

_____

Ephesians 6:1–3 (on obeying parents)

_____

The Sacrament of Matrimony

NAME

Fill in the blanks from the word bank below to complete these statements about marriage taken from the *Catechism of the Catholic Church*.

word	love	grace	consent	dissolved
life	Christ	faithful	children	trial marriages

1. God, who created man out of love, also calls him to _____—the fundamental and innate vocation of every human being.

2. The _____ by which the spouses mutually give and receive one another is sealed by God himself.

3. Thus the marriage bond . . . between baptized persons can never be _____.

4. The covenant that spouses have freely entered into entails _____ love.

5. Fidelity expresses constancy in keeping one's given _____.

6. Human love does not tolerate _____. It demands a total and definitive gift of persons to one another.

7. [The] _____ proper to the Sacrament of Matrimony is intended to perfect the couple's love.

8. _____ is the source of this grace.

9. _____ are the supreme gift of marriage and contribute greatly to the good of the parents themselves.

10. The fundamental task of marriage and family is to be at the service of _____.

100 Activities Based on the Catechism of the Catholic Church
© 1996 Ignatius Press

You and Society

NAME

You probably hear adults discussing social issues or talking about the good or bad aspects of our contemporary society. What exactly is "society"? Is it politics? Is it the media, music, and other parts of popular culture? Do only adults participate? Is it something to which you belong and can make a contribution?

A society is an organized group of individuals who come together for a common purpose that is beyond any one of those individuals. A society can be as small and intimate as a family, or as large and complex as the state or country of which they are citizens.

Since the fall of Adam, original sin has created the potential for harm to individuals through the societies in which they live. Some societies, for example, fail to regard the dignity of each individual person. Through Christ, however, we are redeemed, and in him we can work toward the redemption of the societies in which we live.

Your family, your school, your community, and your sports teams and other clubs are some of the societies to which you belong, and all share some common features. For example, all of them have some form of **authority**, person or people who govern the society and take responsibility for its well-being. Authority is legitimate when it is moral and seeks the good of all. Societies also have a common mission, or **purpose**, which holds them together and focuses the efforts of individuals. Each person has a **duty** to perform within the communities to which he belongs. Finally, everyone has different **talents** and strengths to contribute to the communities to which he belongs, and those are in turn developed within those communities.

On the next page of this activity, describe five of the "societies" to which you belong. For each society, write its name, authority, and purpose, and then your own duties toward each and the talents you bring to each.

You and Society

NAME _____

1. **Family**
   Name: _____
   Authority: _____
   Purpose: _____
   My personal duty: _____
   My talents: _____

2. **School**
   Name: _____
   Authority: _____
   Purpose: _____
   My personal duty: _____
   My talents: _____

3. **Local community**
   Name: _____
   Authority: _____
   Purpose: _____
   My personal duty: _____
   My talents: _____

4. **Club or team (A)**
   Name: _____
   Authority: _____
   Purpose: _____
   My personal duty: _____
   My talents: _____

5. **Club or team (B)**
   Name: _____
   Authority: _____
   Purpose: _____
   My personal duty: _____
   My talents: _____

100 Activities Based on the Catechism of the Catholic Church
© 1996 Ignatius Press

Freedom and Morality

NAME

Made in the image of God, man has a free will. That is, he can control his own thoughts and actions. Because of this innate freedom, man's actions can be morally judged as good or evil. Solve this crossword puzzle, using the clues that explore the various concepts of freedom and morality.

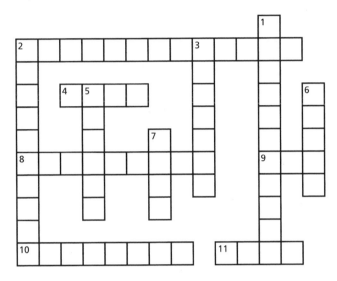

ACROSS

2. The conditions relevant to an act, which affect the moral evaluation of that act. (One of three "sources" of morality of human acts.)

4. One general guideline of morality is that a person may not do evil even if _____ may result from it.

8. A second source of morality, which refers to the purpose in mind of the one committing the act. Synonyms: plan, purpose.

9. To go against the judgment of one's conscience—or what one knows or believes is right—is to _____.

10. Synonym for "feelings" or "passions". They are not moral in and of themselves but can contribute to a good or bad action.

11. Christ has set us _____ from the slavery of sin.

DOWN

1. Because we have free will, we are _____ for our actions.

2. The "inner voice" that helps a person decide if an act is right or wrong.

3. Choices a person makes that can be judged as good or evil are called moral _____.

5. The third source of morality. It is a good toward which the will directs itself, or the thing chosen. Synonymous with "thing".

6. The ends do not justify the _____.

7. A Virtue is a habitual and _____ disposition to do good. Synonyms: strong, unyielding.

The Gospel of Life

NAME

In 1995, Pope John Paul II addressed the bishops, the universal Church, and "all people of good will" with the powerful encyclical letter *Evangelium vitae*, or *The Gospel of Life*. In this challenging statement, which quotes from the *Catechism of the Catholic Church* and reaffirms its teaching, the Pope describes the current threats to human life and calls for a new culture of life based on God's holy law.

In this exercise, give a short answer to questions about selected passages from *The Gospel of Life*. Use a separate paper to write your answers.

1. "Humanity today offers us a truly alarming spectacle, if we consider not only how extensively attacks on life are spreading, but also their unheard-of numerical proportion, and the fact that they receive widespread and powerful support from a broad consensus on the part of society, from widespread legal approval and the involvement of certain sectors of health-care personnel" (chapter 1, no. 17).

   Give an example of the attacks on life the Pope describes.

2. The Pope writes that the loss of a sense of God leads to practical materialism: "The values of being are replaced by those of having. The only goal which counts is the pursuit of one's own material well-being" (chapter 1, no. 23).

   In what ways have you seen this attitude of materialism in our culture?

3. "Through the words, the actions and the very person of Jesus, man is given the possibility of 'knowing' the complete truth concerning the value of human life" (chapter 2, no. 29).

   Give two or more examples from the life of Christ in which he illuminated the value of human life.

4. Upholding the principle stated in the *Catechism* that bloodless means should be used to defend human lives whenever such means are sufficient to protect public order and the safety of persons, the Pope says this about the death penalty: ". . . the nature of and extent of the punishment must be carefully evaluated and decided upon, and ought not go to the extreme of executing the offender except in cases of absolute necessity: in other words, when it would not be possible otherwise to defend society. Today, however, as a result of steady improvements in the organization of the penal system, such cases are very rare, if not practically non-existent" (chapter 3, no. 56).

   What is the Holy Father saying about the death penalty?

5. ". . . I confirm that the direct and voluntary killing of an innocent human being is always gravely immoral. This doctrine, based upon that unwritten law which man, in the light of reason, finds in his own heart (cf. Rom. 2:14–15), is reaffirmed by Sacred Scripture, transmitted by the Tradition of the Church and taught by the ordinary and universal Magisterium" (chapter 3, no. 57).

   List the four means by which we can be certain of the truth of this doctrine.

100 Activities Based on the Catechism of the Catholic Church
© 1996 Ignatius Press

The Gospel of Life

NAME

6. "Among all the crimes which can be committed against life, procured abortion has characteristics making it particularly serious and deplorable. The Second Vatican Council defines abortion, together with infanticide, as an 'unspeakable crime'" (chapter 3, no. 58).

   What makes abortion so morally evil as to be called "unspeakable"?

7. "When the prevailing tendency is to value life only to the extent that it brings pleasure and well-being, suffering seems like an unbearable setback, something from which one must be freed at all costs. Death is considered 'senseless' if it suddenly interrupts a life still open to a future of new and interesting experiences. But it becomes a 'rightful liberation' once life is held to be no longer meaningful because it is filled with pain and inexorably doomed to even greater suffering" (chapter 3, no. 64).

   What value does a Christian find in suffering?

8. "For a correct moral judgment on euthanasia, in the first place a clear definition is required. Euthanasia in the strict sense is understood to be an action or omission which of itself and by intention causes death, with the purpose of eliminating all suffering" (chapter 3, no. 65).

   Which of the following are not *about euthanasia?*

   (a) "To concur with the intention of another person to commit suicide and to help in carrying it out through so-called 'assisted suicide' . . ." (chapter 3, no. 66).

   (b) ". . . 'methods of palliative care,' which seek to make suffering more bearable in the final stages of illness . . . even when the result is decreased consciousness and a shortening of life, 'if no other means exist . . .'" to relieve pain (chapter 3, no. 65).

   (c) The decision to forego medical treatments "which no longer correspond to the real situation of the patient, either because they are by now disproportionate to any expected results or because they impose an excessive burden on the patient and his family . . . when death is clearly imminent and inevitable . . ." (chapter 3, no. 65).

   (d) ". . . when certain people, such as physicians or legislators, arrogate to themselves the power to decide who ought to live and who ought to die" (chapter 3, no. 66).

9. ". . . the *Gospel of Life* is to be celebrated above all in daily living, which should be filled with self-giving love for others" (chapter 4, no. 86).

   What are some ways a person your age can help bring about a "culture of life"?

Speaking the Truth in Love

TEACHER-DIRECTED ACTIVITY

Purpose: to encourage students in the right use of speech in building up one another in Christ.

Hint: This activity is better suited for the second semester, when students are better acquainted. It will take more than one class period.

Directions

Set up in front of the classroom one chair facing the class and, next to that, a desk with chair, also facing the class. At the desk place some notebook paper and a pen.

Ask: Who can tell me what the Eighth Commandment says? [*Elicit the full response: You shall not bear false witness against your neighbor. If the students are a little rusty, you may want to take a few minutes to review the Ten Commandments with them, or to schedule a review at your next opportunity.*] What does it mean to bear false witness? [*To tell a lie, to conceal the truth, and so on.*] We break this commandment every time we commit an offense against truth. The *Catechism of the Catholic Church* actually lists several ways we can break this commandment, ways that we do not always think of.

For example, it is wrong to commit perjury, that is, to break an oath to tell the truth before a judge or jury in a court of law. What harm could come from perjury? [*Guilty person might go free, or innocent person might be found guilty.*]

How about something a little more commonplace. Have you ever heard of "detraction"? That means talking about someone's faults to another person who didn't know of those faults. What harm can come from that? [*Hurts person's reputation, weakens trust between speaker and listener, and so on.*]

How about "rash judgment"? That means you believe without evidence something bad about another person. Why might this be wrong? [*We are accountable to God for our thoughts; Jesus told us not to judge others, for that is how we will be judged.*]

Did you know that boasting, or bragging, also breaks the Eighth Commandment? What does it mean to boast? [*To talk about oneself or one's accomplishments in a proud or vain way.*] Why is that an offense against truth? [*We are all here by the grace of God and are not self-sufficient.*]

Does it seem pretty easy to break the Eighth Commandment? For some people, it can be a real struggle not to do so. Listen to what Saint James said in his letter to the Church: ". . . no human being can tame the tongue—a restless evil, full of deadly poison. With it we bless the Lord and Father, and with it we curse men who are made in the likeness of God." Sad, but true. Yet, James is not without hope, for he goes on to say "this need not be so" (James 3:8–10). As with any struggle against sin, we don't give up, we engage in battle, using the spiritual weapons of the sacraments, prayer, spiritual reading, and spending time with mature Christians.

Now if to break the Eighth Commandment means to bear false witness, to obey the Eighth Commandment must mean to bear *true* witness. We're going to play a game that will give us the chance to do that.

Choose two students, one to be the "candidate" and the other to be the "interviewer". The candidate is to sit in the chair facing the class, and the interviewer will sit in the chair at the desk. The first interviewer should be someone who is comfortable talking in front of the class.

Say: "Jane" is our first candidate. She is running for the "Image of God" award. "Joe" is her interviewer. Everyone will be needed to take part in this game, and everyone will have a turn up here in front.

Joe is going to begin this game by writing down the nicest thing he can think of about Jane to indicate why she should be selected for the "Image of God" award. We'll give him a minute or two. His reason could be a good deed she has done for him or someone else, something about her personality or her character, or whatever it is that he thinks makes her an outstanding image of God. [*When Joe is finished writing, have him read what he wrote to the class.*] Now Joe is ready to do some interviews. He wants to know what every-

Speaking the Truth in Love

one else can say about Jane in favor of her selection as Image of God. The judges like to hear different kinds of statements, so try to say something that has not already been mentioned. Joe will write them all down. All right, raise your hands as you think of something, and Joe will call on you.

Proceed as described. Everyone should participate—after it gets going, this should continue fairly easily, as students will rise to the occasion of praising another.

Say: Now, Joe, you may give this list to Jane. It is hers to keep. I think we can all agree that Jane should win the award! [*Lead applause.*] Now, Jane, it is your turn to be the interviewer, and I would like you to call on the next candidate.

Game proceeds as before. Continue to play until the end of the period, and continue in as many class periods as needed—it may take two or three—until everyone has had a turn as a candidate. It is vital that everyone has a turn, so be sure you have allowed enough time in your schedule. If desirable, this may be done as a "last 10 minutes of class" activity for as many days as there are students.

After everyone has had a chance to receive praise, pass out copies of Activity 96. Ask students to write their answers to the questions in class or at home. Call on various students to share their answers with the class. Allow time for discussion.

Option 1

Teacher can be the interviewer, if class lacks the maturity to conduct this activity.

Option 2

Rather than having the interviewer call on students and record their comments, some time can be given for all the students to write their statements, simultaneously and anonymously, after which the teacher can collect them and selectively read them aloud. Students should be given all positive comments to keep.

Speaking the Truth in Love

NAME

You all have received feedback from your classmates about which qualities you possess that reflect the image of God. Write down the answers to the following questions and discuss them as a class.

1. How did it feel to receive positive comments from your classmates?

   _____

   _____

2. How would you have felt if the comments had been critical or negative?

   _____

   _____

3. Why is it important to receive sincere praise from others?

   _____

   _____

4. Why is it important to give sincere praise to others? And what should be your motive for doing so?

   _____

   _____

5. What is flattery, why is it given, and why is it against the Eighth Commandment?

   _____

   _____

6. Is it ever right or correct to give constructive criticism? When? And what should be the motive or reason for doing so?

   _____

   _____

   _____

   _____

Understanding the "Our Father"

NAME

It has been called "the most perfect of prayers" (Saint Thomas Aquinas), the sum of all the prayers in Scripture (Saint Augustine), and the "summary of the whole gospel" (Church Father Tertullian). The "Our Father", also known as the "Lord's Prayer" because it was given to us by Jesus, holds a unique and honorable place in the life of the Church. We find the Lord's Prayer in the Sunday Mass, in the Liturgy of the Hours, and in the rites of Baptism and Confirmation.

For all its frequent use and familiarity, the "Our Father" was never intended by our Lord to be a mere recitation. When you pray, you should direct your minds and hearts to God so that ". . . you remain in me and my words remain in you . . ." (Jn 15:7).

To increase your understanding of the "Our Father", look up the Bible verses. On a separate sheet of paper, answer the questions.

"Our Father"—Galatians 3:26, 4:6

1. Why do we call the God of the universe "Our Father"?

2. If God is our Father, who are we to each other?

"who art in heaven"—Revelation 7:9–17

3. Using Saint John's vision as a guide, how do you imagine heaven?

"hallowed be thy name"—John 12:27, 28

4. This part of the "Our Father" is the first of seven petitions, or prayerful requests, that make up the rest of the "Lord's Prayer". If we understand this phrase not as praise but as a petition, what are we asking of God?

"Thy kingdom come"—Matthew 25:31–34

5. When we pray this petition, what are we asking for?

"Thy will be done on earth as it is in heaven"—John 13:34

6. What is God's will?

"Give us this day our daily bread"—John 6:5–14, 22–27

7. God satisfies what two types of hunger?

8. What is the "food which endures to eternal life" that Jesus feeds us?

9. This petition also implies responsibilities for Christians. What are they?

"and forgive us our trespasses, as we forgive those who trespass against us"—Matthew 18:23–35

10. This petition is remarkable in that it does not stand alone but comes with a condition, linked by the word "as". Restate the entire petition in your own words.

11. The divine forgiveness Jesus asks of us would be impossible for us to give on our own strength. Who dwells within us to enable us to forgive one another as God has forgiven us?

"and lead us not into temptation"—1 Corinthians 10:13

12. How does God help us in time of temptation?

"but deliver us from evil."—John 17:15

13. In this petition, from whom do we ask to be delivered?

John 17: The Priestly Prayer of Jesus

NAME

The last of Jesus' discourses to his disciples, as written by the evangelist and apostle John (Jn 17), is a prayer, the longest prayer in the Gospels. Called the "prayer of Jesus", or the "prayer of the hour of Jesus", this appeal to his Father unveils the plan of salvation from the beginning of the world to Christ's glory in heaven.

Since the sixteenth century, this chapter has been called the "priestly prayer" of Jesus, who intercedes for his followers as he prepares for his consecration as high priest and sacrifice. Also in this prayer we find echoes of the "Our Father", whose petitions it fulfills.

Read the prayer in your Bibles. Then answer the questions.

1. In which verse does Jesus mention his "hour"? What is his hour?

   _____

2. In which verse does Jesus begin to pray for us, his modern-day disciples?

   _____

3. Which of Jesus' disciples was "lost", as mentioned in verse 12?

   _____

Match the verse from Jesus' prayer on the left with the petition from the "Our Father" that it fulfills on the right.

4. _____ Verses 22–24

5. _____ Verse 15

6. _____ Verses 4 and 26

7. _____ Verse 6

a. "hallowed be thy name"

b. "thy kingdom come"

c. "thy will be done"

d. "but deliver us from evil"

100 Activities Based on the Catechism of the Catholic Church
© 1996 Ignatius Press

Fifteen Minutes with God

TEACHER-DIRECTED ACTIVITY

Materials: Bibles, copies of "Scriptures and Prayer Steps" (see next page), prayer journals (five sheets notebook paper stapled, or three sheets blank paper folded in half and stapled in center like a book).

Purpose: to encourage in students the practice of daily prayer and to introduce them to meditation on the Scriptures as a way to communion with God.

Directions

Distribute Bibles, prayer guidelines (page 112), and blank paper for "prayer journals" to students.

Say: Let's pretend the president of the United States is coming to town, and he wants to put his "finger on the pulse of America", so to speak. He wants to talk to some ordinary citizens to learn what their concerns are, their opinions about current issues, and so on. Your family has been randomly chosen for the visit. In fact, he will be coming over to your house tomorrow, and he wants to have 15 minutes with you, personally, to talk to you about some of his programs and to listen to your hopes and fears about the country. You may even be on the network news for a minute or two.

What would you do to get ready? [*Read recent newspapers, get a haircut, help clean the house, tell your friends, and so forth.*] Now, you're a busy person. You might have to miss a ball practice or music lesson for this. Would you still do it? [*Of course!*] Why? [*He's the president, chance of a lifetime, an honor, and so forth.*]

What if, by some strange turn of events, the president now wants you as a youth adviser, and he wants to be able to talk with you by phone every day, for about fifteen minutes. That's a lot of time out of your life. Would you do it, even if it meant getting up earlier in the morning, or taking some personal time after school? [*Yes.*] Why? [*Great opportunity, lot of influence, and so on.*]

The fact is, there is someone more important, more powerful, and more interested in you than the president, who would like to meet with you every day. That Person is God himself. He wants us to be in touch with him all through the day, but it is hard to do that unless we deliberately set aside a certain time to give him our full attention.

Probably you already have some kind of prayer practice—maybe you say certain prayers at night before sleeping or in the morning to give your day to God. You pray at Mass, and I know you pray before tests! Most of us need help and encouragement to grow in prayer. So, for the next week, I want us all to commit to a fifteen-minute appointment with God for five days between now and when we meet next. [*For classes that meet daily, this can be done in any five- to seven-day period.*] Does fifteen minutes sound like a long time to pray? One five-decade Rosary prayed devoutly takes about that long.

Rather than our formal prayers, we will try meditation, specifically, meditation on the Scriptures. You might have heard of meditation in the context of Eastern religions, but actually there is a long tradition of Christian meditation. On the sheet I've given you are Scriptures for each day and a guideline for your meditation prayer. You also have some blank paper in which to make a prayer journal. Your journal is private. At the end of the week, we'll discuss how our prayer appointments went and what we learned.

Fifteen Minutes with God: Scriptures and Prayer Steps

Day One: Psalm 95:1–7

Day Two: Proverbs 3:13–35

Day Three: Ephesians 3:14–21

Day Four: Psalm 139:1–18

Day Five: Luke 15:11–32

STEP 1
Choose a time and place in which you can have privacy and quiet and can be somewhat alert. Try getting up 15 minutes earlier in the morning.

STEP 2
Invite the Holy Spirit to inspire you as you read and guide you in your prayer.

STEP 3
Read the Scripture passage all the way through, then go back and read the verses more slowly.

STEP 4
Stop at any verse or phrase that seems to "jump out" or have special meaning.

STEP 5
"Listen" to God speak in that verse, or in the whole passage.

STEP 6
Try to "put yourself" in the passage, making the scriptural prayer your own, or envisioning yourself in the scene. Use your imagination to see, hear, or touch what the words describe.

STEP 7
Talk to God about what you've read. There's no need to be formal; be yourself. Write your thoughts, responses, feelings, or prayers in your prayer journal. If it helps you, start the page with "Dear God" or "Dear Jesus".

STEP 8
Be open to any or all of the five forms of prayer: adoration, praise, thanksgiving, petition, and intercession.

STEP 9
Don't worry if you get distracted; it is common. Just turn your attention back to the Lord.

Fifteen Minutes with God: Class Discussion

TEACHER-DIRECTED ACTIVITY

Note: If you meet for class daily, you should remind your students to be keeping their appointments each day. Set an example by keeping yours!

Questions for class discussion

How did your appointments go?

What makes prayer difficult?

What makes prayer rewarding?

Where and when do you like to pray best?

What would help you to continue to pray daily?

Be open to helping students find books or other aids about prayer; many such resources exist. Also, you might suggest that students continue their 15 minutes by prayerfully reading through the Gospels, one chapter a day.

Answer Keys

PRIMARY ACTIVITIES

Activity 1, page 7
1. leaf
2. cat
3. stars
4. fish
5. egg
6. bird

Activity 2, page 8
1. children
2. Heaven
3. holy
4. God's
5. good
6. needs
7. merciful
8. grace
9. hears, strength
10. greater

Activity 3, page 9
Jesus is the **Son** of God.
He came down from **Heaven**.
Christmas is Jesus' birthday.
Her name is **Mary**.
God gave Jesus a **foster** father.
Jesus came to **save** all people from their sins.
Jesus came to bring God's **love**.

Activity 4, page 10
Order of numbers: 8, 1, 5, 6, 2, 4, 3, 9, 7

Activity 5, page 11
"Jesus" means "God saves".

Activity 6, page 12

Activity 7, page 13
the other Mary, angel, happy, Jesus, embraced
"**Do not** be afraid."

Activity 10, page 16
water, prayer book, candle

Activity 11, page 17
Yes, Yes, No, Yes

Activity 12, page 18
altar, vestments, Mass book, host, candles

Activity 14, page 20
mortal, Reconciliation, one hour, food, Communion,
Word, Eucharistic Prayer, "Amen".

Activity 17, page 24
1. Obeyed His parents.
2. Helped the sick.
3. Loved children.
4. Prayed.
5. Gave people food.
6. Told people about God's love.
7. Loved people whom others did not like.

Activity 18, page 25
1. 3
2. 1
3. 2
4. 2
5. 1
6. 3

Activity 19, page 26
1. 8
2. 5
3. 10
4. 4
5. 7
6. 6
7. 9
8. 4
9. 8

Activity 20, page 27
1. c
2. b
3. d
4. e
5. a
6. f
7. g
8. h

Activity 21, page 28
pray, day
food, good
praise, ways
others, brothers
loud, crowd
kneel, real
Be, me
too, you

Activity 23, page 31
Yes

INTERMEDIATE ACTIVITIES

Activity 28, page 36

1. h
2. d
3. g
4. b
5. c
6. g
7. a
8. f
9. e
10. b

Activity 29, page 37

1. e
2. g
3. i
4. j
5. h
6. k
7. a
8. l
9. d
10. f
11. c
12. b

Activity 32, page 40

1. e
2. b
3. f
4. c
5. d
6. g
7. i
8. h
9. a

Activity 33, page 41

1. Father, heaven
2. Son
3. Holy Spirit, Mary
4. crucified
6. third
7. right
8. dead
9. believe, Church, saints
10. sins, life

Activity 34, page 43

1. Father
2. eternally begotten
3. for us men and for our salvation
4. Pontius Pilate
5. suffered, died, and was buried
6. the Scriptures
7. seated at the right hand of the Father
8. in glory

9. With the Father and the Son he is worshiped and glorified.
10. He has spoken through the Prophets.
11. one, holy, catholic, apostolic
12. baptism
13. the resurrection of the dead, the life of the world to come

Activity 38, page 46

1. Omnipotent: All-powerful, almighty, having unlimited power
2. Omniscient: All-knowing, having infinite knowledge
3. Sovereign: Reigning independent of others, above or superior to others, ruling
4. Holy: Spiritually perfect, without sin
5. Just: Right or fair, impartial, upright, lawful, correct
6. Everlasting: Without end, eternal, existing through all time
7. Wise: Having good judgment, making right choices, discerning
8. Faithful: Steadfast, loyal, reliable, dependable, true
9. Good: Virtuous, excellent, pure, correct, desirable

Activity 39, page 47

1. generous
2. kind
3. generous
4. just
5. life-giving
6. wise
7. kind
8. just
9. merciful
10. holy

Activity 40, page 48

1. powerful
2. good
3. knowing
4. male, female, image

Activity 41, page 49

Adam—Sixth
Fish—Fifth
Day—First
Night—First
Eve—Sixth
Stars—Fourth
Trees—Third

Activity 42, page 50

1. False
2. True
3. True
4. True
5. True
6. False
7. True

INTERMEDIATE ACTIVITIES

8. False
9. True
10. False

Activity 43, page 51
1. Saint Michael the Archangel
2. Guardian angel(s)
3. Gabriel

Activity 44, page 52
1. Son
2. Adam
3. Lord
4. Risen
5. Bread
6. Lamb
7. Man
8. Good
9. I Am
10. Light

Activity 45, page 53
1. Pentecost
2. Apostles
3. Mary
4. Abraham
5. Church
6. Holy Spirit
7. water
8. Scripture
9. dove
   The name Jesus used for the Holy Spirit is PARACLETE.

Activity 46, page 54
love
joy
peace
patience
kindness
goodness
faithfulness
gentleness
self-control

Activity 47, page 55
1. O (H)
2. A
3. O (C)
4. H
5. C
6. H
7. O
8. C
9. A
10. H
11. C (O)
12. A

Activity 52, page 59
1. Uncle Henry
2. a. serious (mortal) sin
   b. fast
3. Increases our union with Christ, renews grace from Baptism, removes venial sin, strengthens us against future sin, strengthens our love of God and neighbor, unites us to one another, reminds us of the poor
4. At least once a year (during the Easter season)
5. As often as he is properly disposed and attends Mass, even daily. Communion may be brought to the sick who cannot attend Mass.
6. Because of its link to the Last Supper that Jesus shared with his Apostles, at which he instituted the Eucharist
7. We re-create Jesus' one sacrifice on the Cross. The Eucharist makes present the one true sacrifice.
8. The words of institution or consecration
9. All of our blessings, including forgiveness of sins, redemption, and Christ's sacrifice
10. The priest
11. Adoration, private Holy Hours, Benediction, Exposition of the Blessed Sacrament, bringing of Communion to the sick

Activity 53, page 60
1. P
2. G
3. W
4. R
5. P
6. G
7. R
8. W
9. P
10. R
11. W
12. R
13. W

Activity 54, page 61
1. T
2. T
3. F
4. T
5. T
6. T
7. T
8. F
9. F
10. T
11. F
12. T

Activity 55, page 62
1. b
2. c

INTERMEDIATE ACTIVITIES

3. a
4. c
5. c
6. b
7. c
8. a
9. b
10. a
11. a
12. c

Activity 57, page 64

1. Pray each day.
2. Go to Mass.
3. Read the Bible.
4. Love one another.
5. Obey parents.
6. Teach children.
7. Celebrate together.

Activity 58, page 65

Honor your **father** and your **mother**.
"that your days may be long in the land which the Lord your God gives you."

Activity 59, page 66

First Commandment: I, the Lord, am your God . . . you shall have no other gods besides me.
Second Commandment: You shall not take the name of the Lord your God in vain.
Third Commandment: Remember the sabbath day, to keep it holy.
Fourth Commandment: Honor your father and your mother.
Fifth Commandment: You shall not kill.
Sixth Commandment: You shall not commit adultery.
Seventh Commandment: You shall not steal.
Eighth Commandment: You shall not bear false witness against your neighbor.
Ninth Commandment: You shall not covet your neighbor's wife.
Tenth Commandment: You shall not covet your neighbor's house . . . or anything that is your neighbor's.

Activity 60, page 67

Deuteronomy
1. Brought them out of the land of Egypt, freed them from slavery, led them toward the promised land.
2. To use his name carelessly or as a curse word, to fail to show proper awe and reverence when using God's name.
3. God made it holy because he rested from his labor of creating the world on the seventh day.
4. Yelling angry, mean things at someone; wishing harm upon someone in one's thoughts; hitting.
5. Tell a lie, talk about someone behind his back, gossiping.
6. "Covet" means to desire enviously something that belongs to someone else. Covetousness makes us angry at

God and others, and unhappy and ungrateful with what God has given us. It can lead to other sins, such as adultery, stealing, or killing.

Activity 61, page 68

1. choose
2. obey
3. inner
4. Spirit
5. Commandments
6. ignorance
7. evil
8. sin
9. Church
10. love

Activity 64, page 71

1. Petition
2. Thanksgiving
3. Praise
4. Blessing and adoration
5. Thanksgiving
6. Intercession
7. Blessing and adoration
8. Praise
9. Intercession
10. Petition

Activity 65, page 72

2. After the Lord's Prayer, petition
3. Preparation of the Gifts, blessing/adoration
4. General Intercessions (Prayers of the Faithful), intercession
5. Penitential Rite (Lord, Have Mercy), petition
6. Eucharistic Prayer (Preface), thanksgiving
7. Glory to God, praise
8. Breaking of the Bread (Lamb of God), petition
9. Liturgy of the Word (response after readings) or Dismissal, thanksgiving
10. Preface acclamation (Holy, Holy, Holy), blessing/adoration
11. Eucharistic Prayer (concluding acclamation), praise
12. Eucharistic Prayer (Preface), thanksgiving

Activity 67, page 75

1. a. Jesus calls himself the "Good Shepherd" in the Gospel (Gospel of John).
   b. His sheep!
   c. I don't always know where I'm going and am in need of guidance; God cares for me and protects me from danger, and so on.
   d. Peaceful, hopeful, content, assured, safe.
2. a. Anguished, distraught, suffering, hopeless
   b. Jesus' crucifixion. Verses 7–11, 15, 16, 18–19
   c. Accept any answer.
3. a. Praise (or blessing/adoration)

INTERMEDIATE ACTIVITIES

b. Assembly. Addresses the people of God: Sing to the Lord a new song . . . Give to the Lord you families of nations, and so on.

c. Glory, wondrous deeds, great, highly to be praised, awesome, splendor, majesty, grandeur, king, made the world, governs with equity, rules with justice, constancy

Activity 68, page 77

1. c
2. m
3. h
4. j
5. n
6. e
7. b
8. o
9. l
10. i
11. g
12. k
13. f
14. a
15. d

Activity 69, page 78

Connecting the dots spells "Mary".

Activity 70, page 79

1. the angel Gabriel, the Mother of Jesus
2. original sin
3. personal sin
4. Elizabeth, faith
5. the Holy Spirit, conceived
6. saint
7. true man
8. our Mother, prayers
9. the Cross, heaven

Activity 73, page 82

1. follow, Apostles
2. Pentecost
3. Commandments
4. novena
5. Beatitudes
6. sacraments
7. created, nothing
8. Pentateuch, laws
9. Matthew, Mark, Luke, and John
10. Father, Son, and Holy Spirit
11. descendants, Adam, Eve, Eden
12. True God

ADVANCED ACTIVITIES

Activity 74, page 84

1. d
2. b
3. c
4. j
5. c
6. a
7. f
8. k
9. a or b
10. e
11. g
12. d, f, j

Activity 75, page 85

1. d
2. b
3. e
4. g
5. a
6. f
7. c
8. h

Activity 77, page 86

1. needs food
2. is one
3. has many parts
4. is organized, designed by God
5. is connected, interrelated
6. grows
7. has a head
8. is beloved
9. is pure, beautiful
10. is cherished, cared for
11. is God's building
12. is holy
13. is a dwelling place of God
14. is built upon the foundation of the apostles, prophets, Christ
15. has a (precious) cornerstone

Activity 79, page 87

1. poverty, chastity, obedience
2. hermits
3. virgin
4. religious
5. set apart
6. missionary
7. the world
8. Church
9. example, witness

Activity 83, page 91

1. death of the body (dead)
2. resurrection
3. Baptism
4. particular judgment
5. heaven
6. purgatory or purification
7. hell
8. last judgment
9. new heaven, new earth

Activity 84, page 92

1. h
2. e
3. k
4. a
5. p
6. m
7. b
8. l
9. q
10. n
11. c
12. j
13. f
14. g
15. i
16. o
17. d

Activity 86, page 94

1. April 7
2. December 25 *
3. November 24
4. December 1
5. December 8 *
6. May 26
7. May 16
8. January 7
9. February 21
10. April 5
11. November 1 *
12. August 15 *
13. March 17
14. December 29
15. January 1 *
16. March 25
17. June 9
18. June 2
19. September 8
20. June 14

Activity 88, page 97

1. b
2. c
3. c
4. a
5. a
6. c
7. a
8. b

ADVANCED ACTIVITIES

9. a
10. b

Activity 89, page 98
1. Baptism, Confirmation
2. Baptism
3. Anointing of the Sick
4. Any or all four
5. Baptism, Confirmation
6. Holy Orders

Activity 91, page 100
1. love
2. consent
3. dissolved
4. faithful
5. word
6. trial marriages
7. grace
8. Christ
9. children
10. life

Activity 93, page 103
Across
2. circumstances
4. good
8. intention
9. sin
10. emotions
11. free
Down
1. responsible
2. conscience
3. actions
5. object
6. means
7. firm

Activity 94, page 104
1. Accept any reasonable answer, including legalized abortion, growing acceptance of "assisted suicides" and incidents of euthanasia, cases of infanticide.
2. Accept any reasonable answer.
3. Accept any reasonable answer, including healings, the raising of Lazarus, his ultimate sacrifice on the Cross, and the fact of the Incarnation, in which Christ became man.
4. Should be permitted only if absolutely necessary for the protection of society; modern prison security makes need for death penalty all but obsolete.
5. Natural law, Sacred Scripture, Tradition of the Church, Magisterium.
6. Killing of an innocent, helpless child at request of the child's own mother, who by nature should nurture and protect her child.
7. Suffering can be offered to Christ for remission of sins of

self or others; can increase one's identification with Christ, who suffered on the Cross; can encourage others if endured bravely; and so on.
8. b and c
9. Accept any reasonable answer.

Activity 96, page 108
1. Accept any answer.
2. Accept any answer.
3. Receiving praise helps me to know myself, to love myself, and to recognize that I am created in the image of God.
4. Giving praise helps me to look for the good in others and to recognize that they are created in the image of God. Giving praise is a way to love others. To love someone for his own sake and not for any benefit to myself should be the motive for giving praise.
5. Flattery is untrue or insincere praise. It is against the Eighth Commandment because it is a form of deceit. Flattery is usually given in order to obtain something from someone.
6. Giving correction can sometimes be a moral duty when the soul or welfare of another person is at stake. It is also the responsibility of those with authority—such as parents, teachers, pastors, and civil leaders—who teach, train, or govern others. The motive for giving correction must always be love of the person for his own sake, that is, concern for his welfare.

Activity 97, page 109
1. Through Christ we are God's children.
2. Christians are brothers and sisters in Christ.
3. Accept any reasonable answer.
4. That he make his name holy, or that he glorify his name.
5. For Jesus Christ to return in glory and judge the world.
6. That we love one another as he has loved us.
7. Physical and spiritual.
8. The Eucharist.
9. To share our bread with the hungry; to receive Holy Communion; to bring Communion to those unable to attend Mass.
10. Accept any reasonable answer that relates the forgiveness we ask of God to the forgiveness we grant others, even enemies.
11. The Holy Spirit
12. He keeps us from being tempted beyond our strength and gives us a way out to avoid sin.
13. Satan.

Activity 98, page 110
1. Verse 1; the hour of his death
2. Verse 20
3. Judas Iscariot
4. b
5. d
6. a
7. c

NOTES

NOTES

NOTES

NOTES